B.J. Summers' Guide to Coca-Cola

Identifications ⋅ Current Values ⋅ Circa Dates

"Thirst knows no season" sign, see page 34.

COLLECTOR BOOKS

A Division of Schroeder Publishing Co., Inc.

The current values in this book should be used only as a guide. They are not intended to set prices, which vary from one section of the country to another. Auction prices as well as dealer prices vary greatly and are affected by condition as well as demand. Neither the Author nor the Publisher assumes responsibility for any losses that might be incurred as a result of consulting this guide.

Searching For A Publisher?

We are always looking for knowledgeable people considered to be experts within their fields. If you feel that there is a real need for a book on your collectible subject and have a large comprehensive collection, contact Collector Books.

On the Cover:

Front, from top left; Wall pocket, p. 221, $450.00; Bottle-in-hand decal, p. 40, $25.00; Verbena festoon, p. 41, $1,200.00; Menu girl tray, p. 100, $75.00; Halloween promotional package, p. 108, $20.00; Child's shopping basket, p. 181, $400.00; Cardboard poster, p. 27, $500.00; Santa cut out, p. 199, $65.00. Back: *Alphabet Book of Coca-Cola,* p. 103, $65.00; Fashion girl, p. 40, $5,500.00.

Cover design by Beth Summers
Book design by Terri Stalions

Additional copies of this book may be ordered from:

Collector Books
P.O. Box 3009
Paducah, Kentucky 42002-3009

@$19.95. Add $2.00 for postage and handling.

Copyright: B.J. Summers, 1997

Contents

Dedication. 4
Acknowledgments 5
Pricing. 7
Introduction 8
Signs 9
Calendars 74
Trays 91
Paper Goods. 103
Fans 112
Blotters. 115
Post Cards 117
Ads 118
Bottles 120
Glasses 133
China 135
Art Plates 136
Mirrors 138
Thermometers. 139
Carriers 143
Vending Machines 147
Coolers 150
Radios 152
Clocks. 153
Openers. 159
Knives 162
Ice Picks 163
Ashtrays 164
Lighters 165
Matches 166
Coasters 168
No Drip Protectors . . . 169
Menu Boards 170
Door Pushes 171
Trucks. 172
Toys. 177
Games. 182
Jewelry 189
Clothing 192
Wallets 196
Santas. 197
Miscellaneous. 209

Cardboard cut-out 3-dimensional Santa, see page 200.

Dedication

When I sat down to dedicate this book, three people immediately came to mind. The first two make up one of the nicest couples you could ever have the privilege of knowing, Alfred and Earlene Mitchell. The third person is my wife Beth. It was my extremely good fortune to marry this lovely, talented, warm, and caring lady 29 years ago. She has been a constant source of support and strength for me, in all my endeavors.

So it is with great pleasure I dedicate this book to Alfred and Earlene Mitchell, and my wife, Beth.

Nashville Coca-Cola salesman Felix H. Redmon (center) shown with his brother, John Redmon (left), and the delivery truck driver, Redmond Johnson in a c. 1920 photo. This Nashville Tennessee salesman operated out of a Coca-Cola bottling works located on Church St., owned by the Weil family. After the death of Mr. Weil, Mrs. Weil operated the business for many years. Felix H. Redmon, the salesman, rode in the truck to collect money, but was not allowed to lift drinks. On this particular day, his brother John, who was visiting, rode along to keep him company.

Photo courtesy Kay Smith

Acknowledgments

I would like to extend my sincere thanks to the following people and businesses without whose help this book would have been impossible.

Collector Books
P.O. Box 3009
Paducah, KY 42002-3009

I would like to thank all of the great people at Collector Books that I've had the pleasure of working with. My sincere thanks to Bill, Billy, Jane, and Lisa. To Charley, our great photographer on this project. Gail for all the know how needed to put two boxes of rough material together into a book and, Beth for the great artwork and fantastic cover.

Alfred and Earlene Mitchell
c/o Collector Books
P.O. Box 3009
Paducah, KY 42002-3009

One of the nicest couples you could ever know, who have been collecting since the sixties. They were kind enough to allow us to photograph much of their collection and answer a constant stream of questions. Al and Earlene are very active collectors. They buy, sell, trade, and are very active in collectors' clubs. They may be contacted in care of Collector Books.

Riverside Antique Mall
P.O. Box 4425
Sevierville, TN 37864
Ph 423-429-0100

Located in a new building overlooking the river, this is a collector's heaven. It's full of advertising, with lighted showcases and plenty of friendly help. You need to allow at least half a day for a quick look through this place that sits in the shadows of the Smokey Mountains.

Affordable Antiques Inc.
933 S 3rd St.
Paducah, KY 42001
Ph 502-442-1225

Easy to find on Paducah's I–24 loop, Oliver Johnson usually has some Coke collectibles worth the visit. If you don't find what you need, he can usually locate it for you.

Gary Metz's Muddy River Trading Co.
263 Lakewood Drive
Moneta, VA 24121
Ph 540-721-2091, Fax 540-721-1782

If you are a collector of Coca-Cola you need to know about The Muddy River Trading Co. Gary has a couple of great auctions each year that offer us a chance at both very rare and common collectibles. He also has a good supply of advertising in stock. And all of his merchandise is guaranteed. I've always found him to be extremely helpful and totally honest. I recommend him highly. *See ad in back of book!*

Collector's Auction Service
Rt 2 Box 431, Oakwood Dr.
Oil City, PA 16301
Ph 814-677-6070

Mark Anderton and Sherry Mullen offer a couple of great mail and phone advertising auctions each year. While their main focus is on oil and gas collectibles, there have been a good many Coca-Cola collectibles offered. It is worthwhile to check them out.

Creatures of Habit
406 Broadway
Paducah, KY 42001
Ph 502-442-2923

This business will take you back in time with its wonderful array of vintage clothing and advertising. If you are ever in western Kentucky stop and see Natalya and Jack.

Broadway House Antiques
229 Broadway
Paducah, KY 42001
Ph 502-575-9025

This former clothing store now presents a unique setting for a good general line antique mall. The famous turn-of-the-century author, Irvin S. Cobb, is said to have purchased his first suit at this location. Located conveniently at Third and Broadway on the I–24 loop in downtown Paducah, this mall is easy to find and carries a great selection.

Acknowledgments

The Illinois Antique Center
308 S.W. Commercial
Peoria, IL 61602
Ph 309-673-3354

Situated on the river in downtown Peoria, this remodeled warehouse is full of great advertising. You need to plan on spending the day here. There's always plenty of courteous help for your convenience.

Chief Paduke Antiques Mall
300 S. 3rd St.
Paducah, KY 42003
Ph 502-442-6799

This full-to-overflowing mall is located in an old railroad depot in downtown Paducah with plenty of general line advertising, including good Coke pieces, plus a good selection of furniture. Stop by and see Charley or Carolyn if you're in this area.

Pleasant Hill Antique Mall & Tea Room
315 South Pleasant Hill Rd
East Peoria, IL 61611
Ph 309-694-4040

One day won't be enough time to look through this stuffed-full warehouse mall. Bob Johnson has a great place for collectors. You can shop until you're ready to drop then have a great meal at the tea room conveniently located in the center of the mall. It has plenty of friendly help and multiple cashier stations.

Goodletsville Antique Mall
213 North Dickerson Pike
Goodletsville, TN 37072
Ph 615-859-7002

With over 90 booths under roof you need plenty of time at this store. They feature a good array of antiques and collectibles, and a good supply of advertising.

Antiques, Cards, and Collectibles
203 Broadway
Paducah, Ky 42001
Ph 502-443-9797

Three floors of antiques and collectibles housed in an old historic hardware store in downtown Paducah. Owner Ray Pelley offers a good array of collectibles along with some great Coca-Cola collectibles.

Michael and Debbie Summers
3258 Harrison St.
Paducah, KY 42001

My sincere thanks to my brother and sister-in-law for all their help tracking down collectibles and collectors.

If I have omitted anyone who should be here please be assured it is an oversight on my part and was not intentional.

Edgar Bergen and Charlie McCarthy sign, see page 51.

Light-up neon counter clock, see page 156.

The intent of this book is to help familiarize the collector with current market values. It is not designed to influence or help set those values. There are several factors that affect values, condition and location are probably the two biggest.

Condition should be a prime factor in determining value. If you are buying a collectible that is in good condition the price shouldn't be the same as a mint piece. Unfortunately we all see mint prices being placed on fair and good collectibles almost daily. The prices given in this book reflect the condition of the specific item as stated in each listing.

Location will also play a part in determining value. In the midwest where I live values will generally be less that in the northeast or on either coast. However remember there are always exceptions to every rule.

Rarity will also play a part in the value of a collectible. How often will you see the piece? And how badly do you want it? Will you see it later on down the road at a better price? All of these questions play a part in determining value.

In addition to this book there are several good reference sources on the market to help with buying and pricing. *Schroeder's Antiques Price Guide, Goldstein's Coca-Cola Collectibles, B.J. Summers Value Guide To Advertising Memorabilia,* and *Huxford's Collectible Advertising* all available from Collector Books are excellent reference sources.

Introduction

Coca-Cola fashion girl, see page 40.

No other single product has captured the heart of the American public like Coca-Cola. We all have memories that relate to this magic elixir. It might be a high school ball game with popcorn and Coke, or a date at the local drive-in sharing a cherry Coke. Ever since the days of Dr. J.S. Pemberton and Asa Griggs Chandler, Coca-Cola has provided us with America's favorite soft drink. And even though it has been with us over a century its closely guarded formula has changed little. That is an unusual accomplishment especially for a product that has affected our entire culture.

The Coca-Cola Company has helped launch the career of many fine artists. And has made the work of several accomplished artists familiar in households across the country. Although Norman Rockwell may be best known for his work as a cover illustrator for *Saturday Evening Post,* he also did art work for Coca-Cola. Two prominent examples are the calendars for 1931 and 1932. And who can think of Christmas without the Coca-Cola Santa Claus coming to mind. The artist Haddon Sundblom created the most popular version of the Coca-Cola Santa Claus.

Over the years many soft drinks have come and gone. But Coca-Cola remains a leader due primarily to the proliferation of wonderful advertising and the company's ability to generate a great product.

When I was given the opportunity to compile this book it seemed only natural. I have a particular attachment to collectible advertising. During research for my first book, *Value Guide To Advertising Memorabilia,* I was reacquainted with the huge amount of advertising produced by, or for, the Coca-Cola Company. So while this book has been challenging it has also been a labor of love. It has been my good fortune to meet some great people and see an amazing array of collectibles.

I hope this book in some way will broaden your collecting experience and help acquaint you with the values of those collectibles.

Aluminum die cut "Drink Coca-Cola In Bottles" in script, truck radiator sign, 1920s, 17½"x7½", EX, $335.00. Gary Metz

Bottle hanger, Santa Claus holding a bottle with information card about "Twas the Night Before Christmas," fold out story inside, 1950s, M, $15.00. Mitchell Collection

Bottle hanger, "Ice Cold Coca-Cola King Size," red, white, and green, M, $3.00. Mitchell Collection

America's Fighting Planes, set of 20 scenes of planes in action, price at $50.00 each if set is incomplete, 1940s, EX, $1,200.00. Mitchell Collection

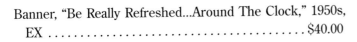

Banner, "Be Really Refreshed...Around The Clock," 1950s, EX $40.00

Banner, canvas, featuring a 24 bottle case with area at bottom for the price, 9' tall, EX. $145.00

Banner, paper, "Home Refreshment," carton at left, 1941, 51"x13", NM $75.00

Banner, paper, "King Size," 1958, 36"x20", NM . $110.00

 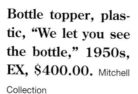

Bottle topper, plastic, "We let you see the bottle," 1950s, EX, $400.00. Mitchell Collection

Bottle hanger, Santa Claus in refrigerator full of bottles being surprised by small child, 1950s, M, $5.00. Mitchell Collection

Bottle topper, woman with yellow scarf and parasol, 1927, 8"x10", VG, $2,000.00. Gary Metz

Banner, "Take Coke Home," 108", EX $150.00

Banner, "Welcome to Super Bowl XXVIII," 102"x34", EX $65.00

Bottle topper, Bathing Girl, "Drink Coca-Cola Delicious and Refreshing," rare, 1929, VG, $1,800.00. Gary Metz

Cardboard advertisement, horizontal, "Have a Coke," woman holding a bottle, 36"x20", EX, $250.00. Gary Metz

Cardboard, 3-D, "Boy oh Boy," pictures boy in front of cooler with a bottle in hand, 1937, 36"x34", VG, $800.00. Mitchell Collection

Cardboard, 3-D, "On Your Break," self-framing, 1950s, $100.00. Mitchell Collection

Cardboard advertisement for a deck of playing cards that can be purchased with six coupons taken from six pack cartons, Piqua Coca-Cola Bottling Company, 1938, 12"x18", $45.00. Mitchell Collection

Cardboard, an African-American family enjoying Coca-Cola, 1958, EX $50.00

Cardboard and wood price board for 6½ oz. and 12 oz sizes with original tin frame, 1950, 25"x15", VG. $145.00

Cardboard and wood right angle display featuring three 6 packs and carriers, "Easy to Carry," carriers have wooden handles, 1947, 42"x33", EX $250.00

Cardboard airplane hangers, complete set of 20 in original envelope, if sold separately price at $35.00 to $50.00 each, 1943, EX, $1,000.00. Mitchell Collection

Cardboard, bather in round blue background, framed and under glass, by Snyder & Black, rare, 1938, 22", NM, $2,000.00. Mitchell Collection

Cardboard, bather in diamond blue background pictured with a Coke button and a bottle, framed and under glass, 1940, 23"x22", NM, $1,400.00. Mitchell Collection

Cardboard bottle display, cut out, featuring a girl in a swimsuit, "So Refreshing," 1930, 9"x17½", VG $475.00

Cardboard bottle display of girl holding tray, 1926, 11½"x14", NM $3,500.00

Cardboard bottle rack, "Enjoy Coca-Cola," 1970–80s, 18", red and white, EX $10.00

Cardboard, boy and girl with bottles, "Coke for me too," 1946, 36"x20", EX . . . . $725.00.

Cardboard carton insert, a lady's hand shown carrying a six pack, "Take Home This Handy 6 Bottle Carton," by Niagara Litho, 1936, G. $85.00

Cardboard carton insert, "Good With Food," 1930s, NM $150.00

Cardboard carton insert, "Refresh Your Guests," 1930, VG $175.00

Cardboard carton insert, "Six for 25¢ Plus Deposit," 1930s, NM $400.00

Cardboard carton insert, slanted red billboard logo "Easy to Serve," 1930, EX $150.00

Cardboard clown balancing on a bottle, 1950, EX, $800.00. Gary Metz

Cardboard, cut, "Buy Coca-Cola Have for Picnic Fun," shows two couples having a picnic, 1950s, EX, $95.00. Mitchell Collection

Cardboard cut out, model with a bottle and a colorful parasol, easel back, 1930s, 10"x18½", EX, $1,500.00. Mitchell Collection

Cardboard cut out, "Drink Coca-Cola, The Pause that Refreshes," used as a window display by Niagara Litho Co. N.Y, 1940s, 32½"x42½", G, $800.00. Mitchell Collection

Cardboard cup sign with Sprite Boy, 1950s, 15"x12", EX $55.00

Cardboard cut out, Athletic Games, 1932, EX. . $55.00

Cardboard cut out, cherub holding a tray with a glass in a glass holder, 14½", EX $3,800.00

Cardboard cut out, couple at sundial, "It's Time to Drink Coca-Cola" on edge of dial, 1911, 29"x36", G . . . $3,500.00

Cardboard cut out, man and woman at sundial, both are holding flare glasses, 1913–1916, 30"x36½", EX . $6,000.00

Cardboard cut out stand up of Eddie Fisher, 1954, 19", EX $225.00

Cardboard cut out, Toonerville, 1930, EX. $80.00

Cardboard cut out, Toy Town, 1927, EX $75.00

Cardboard die cast 3-D, featuring Claudette Colbert, 1933, 10"x20", EX $5,500.00

Cardboard die cut, embossed, WWII battleship, framed under glass, 26"x14", NM, $1,300.00. Gary Metz

Cardboard die cut 6 pack, 1954, 12", NM. $700.00

Cardboard die cut 6 pack with "6 for 25¢" on carton, 1950, 12", NM. $575.00

Cardboard die cut, embossed, easel back Victorian sign promoting Coca-Cola chewing gum, girl in woods, Kaufmann and Strauss Company, New York, framed and matted, 1903–05, 4½"x10½", NM $15,500.00

Cardboard die cut, hand in bottle, "Take Enough Home," companion piece at top, 1952, 11"x14", NM $180.00

Cardboard die cut of lady's face with actual scarf, EX . $125.00

Cardboard die cut, sailor girl, framed under glass, 1952, 11"x7", EX. $375.00

Cardboard die cut, two sided, girl and a glass, 1960s, 13"x17", EX. $425.00

Cardboard die cut window display, 15 piece Toonerville, EX. $275.00

Cardboard die cut with an ice bucket scene and a glass and bottle in front, 1926, EX. $550.00

Cardboard display, "Pick Up The Fixins, Enjoy Coke," 1957, 20"x14", NM $20.00

Cardboard easel back, boy and girl under mistletoe, "Things Go Better With Coke," 1960s, 16"x27", EX $30.00

Cardboard die cut six pack, 1954, EX, $750.00. Gary Metz

Cardboard, die cut, "Take Enough Home," bottle in hand, 1952, VG, $160.00. Gary Metz

Cardboard die cut with attached hangers for wall or window display, Bathing Girl, 1910, F, $1,450.00. Gary Metz

Cardboard, die cut, woman 5' tall, holding six pack, EX, $75.00. Gary Metz

Cardboard easel back, girls on a bicycle built for two, "Extra Fun Takes More than One," 1960s $30.00

Cardboard easel back, Kit Carson advertising bottle sales and Rodeo Tie promotion, 1953, 16"x24", G $250.00

Cardboard easel back, Shopping Girl, 1956, 2½'x5', EX $900.00

Cardboard featuring Eddie Fisher on radio, 1954, 12"x20", EX $65.00

Cardboard festoon backbar display, girl's head, five pieces, 1951, NM $1,100.00

Cardboard, horizontal, "12 oz ice cold," head shot of woman with a bottle, promoting sale of king size products, 1959, 36"x20", EX $225.00

Cardboard, horizontal, "Accepted Home Refreshment," couple with popcorn and Coca-Cola in front of fireplace, "Drink..." button lower right, 1942, 56"x27", G . . . $175.00

Cardboard, horizontal, "Be Really Refreshed," scene of couple in boat on pond, 1960s, 36"x20", EX $85.00

Cardboard, horizontal, "Enjoy the quality taste," girl in swim suit at beach, 1956, 36"x20", EX $255.00

Cardboard, "Drink Coca-Cola," couple on a beach with a large towel, 1932, 29"x50", Hayden-Hayden, F, $600.00. Mitchell Collection

Cardboard, horizontal, "For the taste you never get tired of," beside "Drink..." button, couple in pool, 1960s, 36"x20", EX $175.00

Cardboard, horizontal "Have a Coke," young cheerleader with megaphone and a bottle, "Coca-Cola" button on right, 1946, 36"x20", G $225.00

Cardboard, horizontal, "Here's Something Good!," woman with crown, man in clown suit with bottle, 1950s, 56"x27", G. $200.00

Cardboard, horizontal, in original wood frame, "Coke is Coca-Cola," 1949, 36"x20", EX $675.00

Cardboard, horizontal, "Refreshing," woman in white dress at counter with a bottle, 1949, 56"x27", VG $375.00

Cardboard, horizontal, "Drink Royal Palm Beverages Made from Pure Cane Sugar by the Coca-Cola Bottling Company," 1930s, 17"x11¼", F, $60.00. Gary Metz

Cardboard, girl with a bottle, 1940s, EX, $600.00. Gary Metz

Cardboard, horizontal, "Inviting you to refreshment," EX, $650.00. Gary Metz

Cardboard, horizontal, "Home Refreshment," woman holding a bottle with flowers in the background, 1950s, 50"x29", G, $200.00. Mitchell Collection

Cardboard, horizontal, "Sparkling" bottle in Q of quality in yellow background, original frame, 1957, 36"x20", EX $450.00

Cardboard, horizontal, "That taste-good feeling," man drinking from a bottle with "Drink Coca-Cola Delicious and Refreshing" button left, 1939, 56"x27", VG $1,000.00

Cardboard, horizontal, "The best of taste," "Drink..." button on right, woman in green suit, 1957, 36"x20", G. . $200.00

Cardboard, horizontal, "Welcome aboard," shore scene with "Drink...." button upper right, 1957, 36"x20", EX $265.00

Cardboard, horizontal, "Welcome," man in uniform and woman in yellow dress seated on couch with a bottle, 1943, 56"x27", EX $450.00

Cardboard, "I'm heading for Coca-Cola," woman in uniform getting off airplane, in original wood frame, 1942, 16"x27", VG, $600.00. Mitchell Collection

Cardboard, "Let's watch for 'em," silhouette of running girl, 1950s, 66"x32", NM $800.00

Cardboard litho of circus performers, framed, 1936, 18"x27", EX $250.00

Cardboard horizontal lettered, button right side, "Fountain Service," 1950, 30"x12", $450.00. Gary Metz

Cardboard, "Party Pause," woman in clown suit, 1940s, 36"x20", G, $350.00. Mitchell Collection

Cardboard in wood frame, "Betty," 1914, 30"x38", VG, $2,750.00. Mitchell Collection

Cardboard, "New Family Size too!," Sprite Boy advertising Coca-Cola all on yellow background, 1955, 16"x27", NM $155.00

Cardboard oval, string hung, denoting price, German, 1930s, EX. $95.00

Cardboard page, heavy, from a salesman's manual, rare and somewhat unusual, 12½"x18½", EX $450.00

Cardboard, "Popcorn Delicious with Ice Cold Coca-Cola," open box of popcorn on its side with Coca-Cola bull's eye at right, 1950s, 15"x12", EX. $200.00

Cardboard poster, 5¢, framed under glass, 1930, 15"x12", EX $210.00

Cardboard poster, "At Ease... for refreshment," military nurse in uniform holding a bottle, in original wooden frame, 1942, NM $1,000.00

Cardboard poster, Bathing Girl on rocks at beach, 1938, 30"x50", G $2,300.00

Cardboard light pulls with original strings advertising King Size Coca-Cola, (left) two sided, 1950–60s, M, $35.00; (right) in six pack, "puts you at your sparkling best," round, M, $30.00. Mitchell Collection

Cardboard, "Pause," clown and an ice skater, in original wooden frame, 1930s, EX, $800.00.
Gary Metz

Cardboard poster, cameo, Lillian Nordica, 1905, F, $9,000.00.

Cardboard poster, "Big Refreshment," girl with bowling ball, 1960s, 66"x32", NM $650.00

Cardboard poster, bird on bell and bottle, in aluminum frame, 1954, EX $250.00

Cardboard poster, "Coke Time," cover girl with original frame, 1950s, 16"x27", NM $750.00

Cardboard poster, couple advertising six pack, framed and matted, 1940s, 16"x27", F $350.00

Cardboard poster, die cut with food scene and bottles, 1939, 31"x42", VG $350.00

Cardboard poster, double sided, "Have A Coke" and Skater Girl on one side with "Refresh Yourself" with horses and riders, 1955, 16"x27", VG $200.00

Cardboard, "Play Refreshed," woman on a carousel horse, in original wooden frame, 1940s, EX, $1,200.00. Gary Metz

Cardboard poster, double sided, one side "the Best of Taste," the other side "Enjoy the Quality Taste," 1956, 56"x27", VG $220.00

Cardboard poster, "Coke Time," woman in cowboy hat and western neck scarf with bottle in hand framed by brands, 1955, G, $225.00.

Mitchell Collection

Cardboard poster, girl on lifeguard stand, 1929, 17"x29¾", VG, $1,000.00. Gary Metz

Cardboard poster, horizontal, "All set at our house," with boy holding cardboard six pack carrier, 1943, EX, $650.00. Gary Metz

Cardboard poster, easel back, "Refresh Yourself," girl on chair with glass, 1926, 16"x29½", EX. $1,500.00

Cardboard poster, "Easy To Take Home," 1941, EX. $350.00

Cardboard poster, Elaine with glass, same art work that was used on the calendar of this year, 1915, EX $3,000.00

Cardboard poster, girl against a rock wall resting from bicycle riding, from Niagara Litho, 1939, VG $375.00

Cardboard poster, girl with a menu and a bottle, 1960s, 66"x32", NM $650.00

Cardboard poster, "Have A Coke," a bottle against an iceberg, 1944, 36"x20" $275.00

Cardboard poster, horizontal, "Be really refreshed...Enjoy Coke"/"Take Home Plenty of Coke," with scene at swimming pool, 1959, 21½"x37½", G, $150.00.

Cardboard poster, horizontal, "Coke knows no season," snow scene with a bottle in foreground and a couple of skiers in the background, framed, 1946, 62"x33", G, $200.00.

Cardboard poster, horizontal, "Coke for me, too," couple with bottles and a hot dog, 1946, 36"x20", EX, $185.00. Gary Metz

Cardboard poster, horizontal, "Coca-Cola belongs," featuring couple with a picnic basket and a bucket of iced Coca-Cola, 1942, EX, $750.00. Gary Metz

Cardboard poster, horizontal, "Coke belongs," young couple with a bottle, 1944, EX, $700.00. Gary Metz

Cardboard poster, horizontal, "Coke Time join the friendly circle," people in pool around cooler on float, 1955, 36"x20", EX, $375.00. Gary Metz

Cardboard poster, horizontal, "Be Really Refreshed," 1950s, EX $90.00

Cardboard poster, horizontal, "Coke belongs," 1940s, 36"x20", EX. $150.00

Cardboard poster, horizontal, "Have a Coke," 1944, 36"x20", EX. $160.00

Cardboard poster, horizontal, "Face your job refreshed," woman wearing visor beside a drill press, 59"x30", VG, $600.00.

Cardboard poster, horizontal, "Got enough Coke on ice?," three girls on sofa, one with phone receiver, framed, Canadian, 1945, G, $250.00.

Cardboard poster, horizontal, "Hello Refreshment," woman in swimsuit coming out of swimming pool, 1940s, 36"x20", EX, $1,700.00. Gary Metz

Cardboard poster, horizontal, "Here's to our G.I. Joes," 1944, VG, $750.00. Gary Metz

Cardboard poster, horizontal, "Hospitality in your hands," woman serving four bottles from tray, 1948, 36"x20", EX, $250.00. Gary Metz

Cardboard poster, horizontal, "Have a Coke," a bottle in snow, 1945, 36"x20", G. $125.00

Cardboard poster, horizontal, "Have a Coke," cheerleader and a bottle, 1946, EX $350.00

Cardboard poster, horizontal, "Hospitality Coca-Cola," girl lighting a candle with a bottle in foreground, 1950, 59"x30", VG, $700.00.

Cardboard poster, horizontal, "He's Coming Home Tomorrow," woman in head scarf and coat with a picnic basket and a bottle, 1944, NM $1,250.00

Cardboard poster, horizontal, "Hello - Coke," couple with bottles, 1944, 36"x20", EX $325.00

Cardboard poster, horizontal, "Lunch Refreshed," 1943, EX, $1,000.00. Gary Metz

Cardboard poster, horizontal, "Now! for Coke," trapeze artist reaching for a bottle, framed, 1959, 27"x21", VG, $300.00.

Cardboard poster, horizontal, majorette, "Refresh," 1952, 36"x20", VG, $475.00. Mitchell Collection

Cardboard poster, horizontal, "Play refreshed," woman in cap with fishing rig and a bottle, 1950s, 36"x20", VG, $300.00. The Mitchell Collection

Cardboard poster, horizontal, "Me too," young boy looking up at large bottle, two sided, 62"x33", G, $450.00.

Cardboard poster, horizontal, "I'll bring the Coke," girl on phone at the foot of stairs, 1946, 36"x20", EX $210.00

Cardboard poster, horizontal, Italian, woman with a bottle, 1940s, 36"x20", EX $425.00

Cardboard poster, horizontal, "Refreshing," pretty girl holding sunglasses and a bottle, in a reproduction frame, 1948, EX, $675.00. Gary Metz

Cardboard poster, horizontal, "Shop refreshed," 1948, EX $1,400.00

Cardboard poster, horizontal, "The answer to thirst," 1945, 36"x20", G $70.00

Cardboard poster, horizontal, "The drink they all expect," couple getting ready to entertain with finger sandwiches and iced bottles, 1942, NM, $600.00. Gary Metz

Cardboard poster, horizontal, "The pause that refreshes," girl in yellow dress propped against table holding a bottle, in a reproduction frame, 36"x20", EX, $900.00. Gary Metz

Cardboard poster, horizontal, "The rest-pause that refreshes," three women in uniform, 1943, 36"x20", EX, $425.00. Gary Metz

Cardboard poster, horizontal, "They all want Coca-Cola," girl delivering a tray with four hamburgers, framed under glass, 36"x20", EX, $130.00. Gary Metz

Cardboard poster, horizontal, "The pause that refreshes," girl on a chaise holding a bottle, 1942, 36"x20", VG, $95.00. Gary Metz

Cardboard poster, horizontal, with Coke cap, 66"x32", EX $800.00

Cardboard poster, horizontal, "Why grow thirsty," 1945, 36"x20", VG. $150.00

Cardboard poster, horizontal, "Zing together with Coke," party scene and cooler on table, 1962, 37"x21", G . $200.00

Cardboard poster, horizontal, "Thirst knows no season," woman drinking from a bottle in front of skiers, framed, 1940, 56"x27", EX, $450.00. Gary Metz

Cardboard poster, horizontal, "To be refreshed," girl holding a bottle in each hand, in reproduction frame, 1948, EX, $325.00. Gary Metz

Cardboard poster, horizontal, "What I want is a Coke," girl on sandy beach in swim suit reaching for a bottle, in original wooden frame, hard to find, 1952, $1,100.00.

Cardboard poster, horizontal, "Welcome Home," 1944, 36"x20", VG, $300.00. Gary Metz

Cardboard poster, "It's a Family Affair," family holding
Coca-Cola, 1941, 36"x20", EX $675.00

Cardboard poster, "It's Twice the Time, Twice the Value,"
1960, 66"x32", NM $800.00

Cardboard poster, Jeff Gordon Coca-Cola 600, 23"x33",
M $10.00

Cardboard poster, large horizontal, "America's Favorite Moment," a couple in a diner booth, each with a bottle, 1940s, 36"x20", EX, $250.00. Gary Metz

Cardboard poster, "Just a Drink But What a Drink," girl
in bathing attire on lifeguard stand, 1929, 17"x29¾",
F. $300.00

Cardboard poster, large horizontal, "Good Pause Drink Coca-Cola in Bottles," 1954, 36"x20", G, $500.00. Mitchell Collection

Cardboard poster, large vertical, "Drink Coca-Cola 50th anniversary," two women in period dress of 1886 and 1936 sitting together, 1936, 27"x47", VG, $475.00. Gary Metz

Cardboard poster, large horizontal, "The pause that refreshes at home," framed, 1940s, 56"x27", EX, $375.00. Gary Metz

Cardboard poster, large horizontal, "a Coke belongs," young boy and girl with a bottle, in original Coke frame, 1944, EX $950.00

Cardboard poster, large horizontal, "Accepted Home Refreshment," couple in front of warm fireplace, 1942, G $725.00

Cardboard poster, large horizontal, couple at open refrigerator with bottles, "Welcome Home," 1944, EX . . . $450.00

Cardboard poster, large horizontal, girl on beach in original Coke frame, 1953, EX $1,250.00

Cardboard poster, large vertical, a soldier and a girl with bicycles and bottles, in original wooden frame, 1943, G $375.00

Cardboard poster, Lillian Nordica, "Coca-Cola Delicious and Refreshing 5¢," standing beside Coca-Cola table with her hand resting on screen at rear of room, rare, 1904, 26"x40", EX, $9,000.00.

Cardboard poster, "The best is always the better buy," girl with grocery sack and six pack, framed under glass, 1943, EX, $975.00.
Gary Metz

Cardboard poster, vertical, "For the party," soldier and woman on bicycle for two, 29"x50½", EX, $425.00. Gary Metz

Cardboard poster, vertical, "Coke headquarters," 1947, EX, $350.00. Gary Metz

Cardboard poster, "On The Refreshing Side," 1941, 30"x50", VG. $375.00

Cardboard poster, part of "Through the Years," Victorian advertising series, 1939, 16"x27", NM. $950.00

Cardboard poster, "Play Refreshed," tennis girl sitting on drink box holding a bottle, in reproduction frame, 1949, 16"x27", G $475.00

Cardboard poster, Reece Tatum of the Harlem Globetrotters holding a basketball with a bottle on top of the ball, 1952, 16"x27", EX. $700.00

Cardboard poster, "Refreshing," girl in water, 1960, 36"x20", EX. $75.00

Cardboard poster, seated Chinese girl, 1936, 14½"x22", NM. $1300.00

Cardboard poster, "Serve Coke At Home," 1949, EX . $300.00

Cardboard poster, "So Delicious," snow ski scene, 1954, 36"x20", VG. $575.00

Cardboard poster, "Now! King Size too!," Sprite Boy with a six pack of king size Coca-Cola and a six pack of regular Coca-Cola, 1955, 16"x27", G, $85.00. Mitchell Collection

Cardboard poster, large vertical, couple and man in navy uniform, 1943, G. $775.00

Cardboard poster, vertical, "Coke Time," head shot of woman, bottle in hand, and various sports activities, 1950s, F, $200.00. Mitchell Collection

Cardboard poster, vertical, double sided, old man north on one side and bottles on the other, French Canadian, 16"x27", $150.00. Gary Metz

Cardboard poster, vertical, "Drink Coca-Cola Delicious and Refreshing," cowboy holding a bottle, 1941, 16"x27", G, $400.00.
Mitchell Collection

Cardboard poster, vertical, "Coke Time," in original wooden frame, 1943, EX, $950.00. Gary Metz

Cardboard poster, "So Refreshing," boy and girl by pool, 1946, 30"x50", EX $675.00

Cardboard poster, vertical, "Drink Coca-Cola," Hostess Girl, 1935, 30"x50", G, $225.00. Gary Metz

Cardboard poster, vertical, "Drink Coca-Cola" in upper left hand corner, girl on towel at beach with a bottle, framed under glass, rare and hard to find, 1930s, 30"x50", EX, $1,700.00. Gary Metz

Cardboard poster, vertical, "Drink Coca-Cola" on button, girl at a stadium in the fall holding a program and a bottle, framed under glass, 1940, 30"x50", EX, $1,400.00.
Gary Metz

Cardboard poster, vertical, "Extra-Bright Refreshment," couple at party holding bottles, 33"x53", G, $200.00.

Cardboard poster, vertical, "Entertain your thirst," two ballerinas at a green bench, framed under glass, 1942, 16"x27", VG, $600.00. Gary Metz

Cardboard poster, Sprite Boy of Woolworth, PA, 11"x14", EX $55.00

Cardboard poster, "The Best of Taste," girl being offered a bottle, 1956, EX $225.00

Cardboard poster, "Tingling Refreshment," girl with a glass waving, 1931, 21"x38", VG. $350.00

Cardboard poster, vertical, "Have a Coke, Coca-Cola," couple at masquerade ball, framed under glass, rare item, F, $550.00.

Cardboard poster, vertical framed, "Home Refreshment on the way," 24½"x50", VG, $275.00. Gary Metz

Cardboard poster, vertical, "Face the sun refreshed," pretty girl in white dress shielding her eyes from the sun with one hand while holding a bottle with the other, 1941, 30"x53½", VG, $500.00.

Cardboard poster, vertical, "Home refreshment," woman holding a bottle with the refrigerator door ajar, 1950s, 16"x27", NM, $550.00. Gary Metz

Cardboard poster, vertical, "Have a Coke," girl with bottle in each hand in front of drink machine, 1940s, 16"x27", EX, $260.00. Gary Metz

Cardboard poster, vertical, "And Coke Too," 1946, 16"x27",
EX $325.00

Cardboard poster, vertical, couple, woman in swim suit
with large brim hat, 1934, 29"x50", EX $2,700.00

Cardboard poster, vertical, "For People on the Go," 1944,
16"x27", G $250.00

Cardboard poster, vertical, "Join me," fencer resting against a chest cooler with a bottle, in reproduction frame, 1947, 16"x27", EX, $775.00. Gary Metz

Cardboard poster, vertical, "Let's have a Coke," cooler and majorette, 1946, 16"x27", EX, $250.00. Gary Metz

Cardboard poster, vertical, mother and daughter at table opening bottle, French Canadian, 1946, 16"x27", $235.00. Gary Metz

Cardboard poster, vertical, "Nothing refreshes like a Coke," couple on bicycles, 1943, EX, $1,700.00. Gary Metz

Cardboard poster, vertical, French Canadian, 1947, 16"x27", VG............................... $230.00

Cardboard poster, vertical, "Happy Ending to Thirst," 1940s, 16"x27", VG.......................... $250.00

Cardboard poster, vertical, "Home Refreshment," framed under glass, EX........................... $1,800.00

Cardboard poster, vertical, "Just Like Old Times," 1945, 16"x27", EX............................... $300.00

Cardboard poster, vertical, man and woman advertising bottle sales, 1930–40s, 18"x36", VG........... $625.00

Cardboard poster, vertical, man in uniform and girl walking each with a bottle, 1944, NM............... $1,250.00

Cardboard poster, vertical, "On the refreshing side," couple with bottles, 1941, 30"x50", VG, $575.00. Gary Metz

Cardboard poster, vertical, "Refreshment," pretty girl in fancy dress at a pool setting with bottles on table, 1949, 33½"x54", VG, $450.00.

Cardboard poster, vertical, "Refreshment right out of the bottle," girl with skates drinking from a bottle, 1941, EX, $750.00. Gary Metz

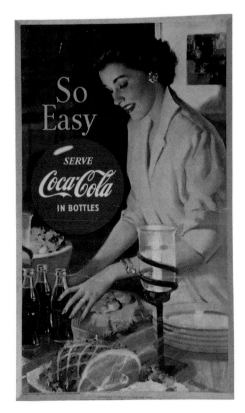

Cardboard poster, vertical, "Right off the ice," girl at ice skating rink, 1946, 16"x27", EX, $210.00. Gary Metz

Cardboard poster, vertical, "So Easy," woman illuminated by candle getting ready for small gathering, 1950s, VG, $375.00. Mitchell Collection

Cardboard poster, vertical, "Play Refreshed," 1949, EX. $750.00

Cardboard poster, vertical, same scene that appears on the 1936 serving tray, the Hostess, framed and under glass, 1935, Hayden, G $700.00

Cardboard poster, vertical, "Start Refreshed," couple at roller skating rink, 1943, 16"x27", VG, $300.00. Gary Metz

Cardboard poster, vertical, "Welcome Pause," girl in yellow with tennis racquet at chest vending machine, 1940s, 16"x27", $260.00. Gary Metz

Cardboard poster, vertical, "The drink they all expect," similar to horizontal poster of this year but showing full length art work of couple preparing for entertaining, 1942, EX, $700.00. Gary Metz

Cardboard poster, vertical, "Take some home today," in original wooden frame, 1950s, 16"x27", VG, $600.00. Gary Metz

Cardboard poster, vertical, "Thirst knows no season," couple building a snowman, graphics are great, 1942, 30"x50", NM, $700.00. Gary Metz

Cardboard poster, vertical, "Talk about refreshing," girl in rain with umbrella in front of cooler holding a bottle, 1942, 16"x27", NM $700.00

Cardboard poster, "Wherever thirst goes," great graphics of girl in row boat with a bucket of iced Coca-Cola, 1942, EX, $475.00. Gary Metz

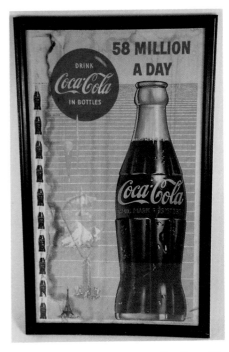

Cardboard poster, vertical, with large bottle in foreground and places and events in background, "58 Million a Day," 1957, 17½"x28½", F, $75.00.

Cardboard poster, vertical, woman sitting on a dock with a parasol behind her holding a glass, "7 million drinks a day," 1926, 18"x31", VG, $1,500.00. Gary Metz

Cardboard poster, woman sitting wearing a broad brimmed hat with flowers, holding a Coca-Cola 5¢ bamboo fan and a glass, framed, 1912, EX, $4,500.00.

Cardboard poster, "Wherever you go," travel scenes in background, 1950s, EX, $175.00. Mitchell Collection

Cardboard poster, vertical, two sided, bottle on one side and target and bottle on the other side, French Canadian, 1951, EX $190.00

Cardboard poster, "Welcome Aboard," nautical theme, 1958, 36"x20", NM $375.00

Cardboard rack display, vertical, "Take more than one," 1960s, 16"x27", EX $85.00

Cardboard, red-head woman in yellow scarf with cup of Coca-Cola, in original aluminum frame, 1951, 13"x11", NM $650.00

Cardboard poster, "Yes," girl on beach with bottle, if found in original frame add $400.00 to this price, 1946, 56"x27", EX, $450.00. Mitchell Collection

Cardboard poster, "Zing-For your supper with ice cold Coke," young cartoon man in early version space suit with food and a bottle, 1960s, $85.00.

Mitchell Collection

Cardboard, St. Louis Fair, woman sitting at table with a flare glass that has a syrup line, 1909, F, $4000.00.

Cardboard, "Serve Yourself," hand in cup, in original aluminum frame, 1951, 13"x11", NM $350.00

Cardboard, stand up, Jeff Gordon & Coke, 1995, NM. $95.00

Cardboard store display, inside, featuring girl in roses, 1937, 52"x34", Haydon Haydon, EX $4,000.00

Cardboard, stand up, "For the emergency shelf," folds in middle, EX, $275.00. Gary Metz

Cardboard trolley car sign featuring a woman sitting off the side of a hammock holding a glass, 1912, EX . . $3,100.00

Cardboard trolley car sign, "Tired? Coca-Cola Relieves Fatigue," young man at dispensers, 1907, VG . . $1,500.00

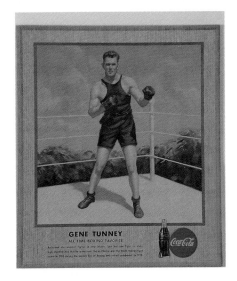

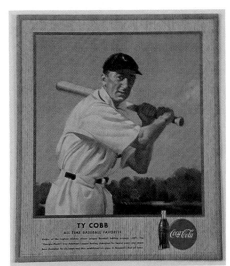

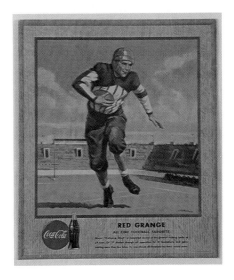

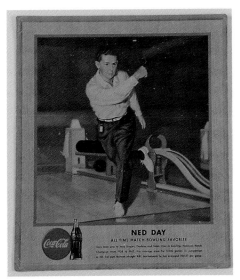

Cardboard, sports favorite, hanging, complete set consists of 10 signs; individual signs go in the $85.00–$110.00 range, 1947, EX, $1,300.00. Mitchell Collection

Cardboard trolley sign, "Drink Coca-Cola Delicious and Refreshing," if mint the value would increase to the $2,000.00 range, 1914, F, $400.00. Mitchell Collection

Cardboard two-piece set, display sign and a paper window banner, "We sell Coca-Cola part of every day - Served ice cold," printed by Snyder & Black, 1942, EX, $425.00. Mitchell Collection

Cardboard, "Welcome friend," red and white lettering on simulated oak background, 1957, 14"x12", EX, $135.00. Mitchell Collection

Cardboard, vertical, "Be Really Refreshed...Enjoy Coke!," woman at beach picnic with a bottle, 1959, 16"x27", EX.............................. $185.00

Cardboard, vertical, "Be Really Refreshed," girl in party dress, "Drink..." button in lower left, 1960s, 16"x27", EX...................................... $185.00

Cardboard, vertical, "Coke Time," bottle in hand with woman's face, "Drink..." button in lower center, 1954, 16"x27", EX............................... $275.00

Cardboard, vertical, "Come and get it," farm bell and a bottle, "Drink..." button in lower right, in original wooden frame, 1954, 16"x27", EX.................... $300.00

Cardboard, vertical, "Come and get it," western dinner gong behind a bottle, "Drink..." button in lower right, 1952, 16"x27", EX......................... $225.00

Cardboard, vertical, "For Holiday Entertaining," six bottle carton 36¢, featuring Christmas decor, Canadian, 1950, 12½"x18½", EX $85.00

Cardboard, vertical, "Now Coke in handy Plastic Cartons," eight pack, easel back, 1960s, 16"x27", EX....... $55.00

Cardboard, vertical poster, with girl on ping pong table, framed under glass, Canadian, 14"x28", EX $600.00

Cardboard, vertical, "So Refreshing," Autumn Girl in art work, 1940, 16"x27", VG $425.00

Cardboard, vertical, "The pause that refreshes," couple with bottles, "Drink..." button over woman's head, in original wooden frame, 1959, 16"x27", G $350.00

Cardboard window display, die cut, depicting a circus, large center piece is 4'x3', a separate girl and ring master is approx. 30" tall, three scenes, clown at big top, vendors and tents, ringmaster and girl, 1932, EX........ $4,600.00

Cardboard window display, cameo fold out, 1913, VG, $5,200.00. Gary Metz

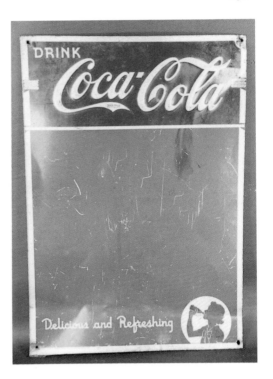

Chalkboard, painted metal, made in U.S.A, American Art Works Inc. Coshoctin, Ohio, 1940, 19¼"x27", F, $25.00.

Celluloid, hand in bottle, foreign, 6½"x16", VG, $225.00. Gary Metz

Celluloid bottle, "Drink Coca-Cola Delicious and Refreshing," 1900, 6"x13¼", VG, $1,800.00.

Celluloid round, "Coca-Cola," white lettering on top of a bottle in center with red background, 1950s, 9" dia, EX, $175.00.

Cardboard window display, tri-fold, Wallace Berry and Jackie Cooper sitting in director's chairs with a bottle in between them, 1934, 43"x31½", VG $2,750.00

Celluloid, round, hanging on easel back, "Delicious Coca-Cola Refreshing," white and black lettering on red background, 1940, EX $180.00

Decal, "Drink Coca-Cola Ice Cold," 1960, EX. $35.00

Decal, "Drink Coca-Cola In Bottles," mounted on glass, 1950s, 15"x9", NM $80.00

Coca-Cola fashion girl, one of four fashion girls, framed and under glass, 1932, EX, $5,500.00. Mitchell Collection

Decal, bottle in hand, EX $25.00

Decal, paper, unused, "Drink Coca-Cola Ice Cold," bottle in shield, 1934, 18"x15", EX, $130.00. Gary Metz

"Drink Coca-Cola, Cures Headache...Relieves Exhaustion at Soda Fountains 5¢," framed under glass, 1890–1900s, VG, $1,000.00. Gary Metz

Decal, "Drink Coca-Cola in Bottles," on glass, framed, 1950s, 15"x18", EX $85.00

Decal, "Drink Coca-Cola In Bottles," red background with white and yellow lettering, 1950s, 16"x8", EX $80.00

Decal, "Drink" emblem on triangle, "Ice and Cold" by bottle, 1934, 15"x18", NM $150.00

Decal, "Drink," fishtail logo, foil, NM $15.00

Decal, "Enjoy That Refreshing New Feeling," fishtail logo, M $30.00

Festoon, state tree complete with original display envelope, 1950s, EX, $400.00. Mitchell Collection

Decal, fishtail logo with sprig of leaves, EX $30.00

Decal, Sprite Boy looking around a large bottle, 13"x13",
   EX $300.00

Decal, "Thank You Come Again," on bow tie emblem, foil,
   1950s, NM. $20.00

Decal, "Things Go Better With Coke," 1960, NM . . . $25.00

Decal, white background, has been sanded down and
   reworked, 1950s, 24", NM. $275.00

Easel back lunch counter sign, 1960s, 12"x17" $65.00

Festoon, autumn leaves, 1922, NM. $1,500.00

Festoon, leaf pattern with girl in center, five pieces with
   original envelope, 1927, NM $4,000.00

**Festoon, verbena, center piece only shown, price
is for complete 5-piece set with ribbons,
$1,250.00.**

Festoon, locket, five pieces with original envelope, 1939,
   NM $1,100.00

Festoon, petunia, five pieces with original envelope, 1939,
   NM $1,100.00

Festoon, people in period dress from 1886 to 1951, pictured is the center piece only, 1951, NM, $1,200.00. Gary Metz

Festoon, two sided, "The Pause that Refreshes," five piece, 1930s, VG, $775.00. Gary Metz

Festoon, snow bough and icicle, five pieces, in original envelope, 1937, NM $4,500.00

Fiberboard, round, pressed and raised, by Kay Displays, scarce, 13" dia, G, $600.00. Gary Metz

Festoon, swan, five pieces with original envelope, 1938, EX $1,800.00

Festoon, theme of parasols, 1918, NM $1,200.00

Festoon, wild rose, five pieces with original envelope, 1938, VG $850.00

Festoon, wood flower, three pieces with original envelope, 1934, NM $900.00

Glass, decal mounted on glass and framed, Sprite Boy, advertising bottles sales, note bottle cap hat as opposed to fountain hat, 13"x13", NM $375.00

Glass and metal light-up, "Work safely work refreshed," cardboard insert, with original packing box, 1950s, 16"x16", EX, $675.00. Gary Metz

Light-up, plastic and glass, "Pause and Refresh," "Quality carries on" on right side with bottle in hand, same art work as appears on fans of this vintage, 1940s, 19"x15½", EX, $650.00.

Glass, oval, "Drink Coca-Cola 5¢," silver lettering on maroon colored background, 1906, 9"x6¾", VG, $2,000.00.

Glass, round, "Drink Coca-Cola 5¢," gold trademark with blue background, 1900s, 8" dia, F, $2,000.00.

Glass, round mirror, "Drink Carbonated Coca-Cola 5¢ in Bottles," G, $400.00. Mitchell Collection

Glass front light-up, "Have a Coke" with cup at right, 1950s, 17"x10", EX $1,400.00

Glass front light-up, metal frame, "Lunch With Us," 1950s, 18"x8", EX................................. $675.00

Glass front light-up, "Please Pay When Served," located on top of courtesy panel, 1950s, 18" x 8", EX $550.00

Glass light-up, 20oz. bottle, 1994, EX............. $140.00

Glass light-up, hanging, "Have A Coca-Cola," 1948, 20"x12", EX $400.00

Glass light-up, NOS, Coca-Cola Beverage Department, fishtail, 1960s, 50"x14", M $300.00

Glass light-up, hand and bottle, probably an independent sign made by a bottler, unusual, 14"x10½", EX. $1,200.00

Glass light-up, "Have A Coke, Refresh Yourself" with red arrow, 1950s, 10"x17", NM................... $1,200.00

Light-up counter top, motion wheel behind "Pause" at left of "Drink Coca-Cola" with "Please Pay Cashier" at bottom, 1950s, M $900.00

Light-up, plastic, rotating, "Shop Refreshed Drink Coca-Cola," 1950s, 21" tall, $525.00. Gary Metz

Light-up, plastic and metal, round, double sided, "Drink Coca-Cola sign of Good Taste," 1950, 16" dia, EX, $550.00. Gary Metz

Masonite and aluminum cooler sign with arrow through outside circle, 1940s, M, $475.00. Mitchell Collection

Light-up, plastic with metal base, "Drink Coca-Cola, Sign of Good Taste," 1950s, VG, $400.00. Mitchell Collection

Light-up, plastic and metal display, "Always a Party, Always Coca-Cola," for Superbowl XXVII, NM $40.00

Light-up, plastic, double sided, hanging, 1950s, 16" dia, EX $450.00

Light-up, plastic with metal base, "Shop Refreshed," "Drink Coca-Cola," 1950s, EX $425.00

Light-up "Beverage Department" with fishtail logo, 1960s, 50"x14" $300.00

Light-up, cash register top, "Drink Coca-Cola, Lunch With Us," 1940–50s, 11"x6", NM $325.00

Light-up, lantern on stand with four panels, "Have a Coke Here" on two panels and fishtail "Drink Coca-Cola" on other panels, 1960s, NM $100.00

Light-up, red two-sided globe hanger, 1950–60, 16" dia, EX $400.00

Masonite, "Delicious & Refreshing," girl with bottle, 1940s, EX $95.00

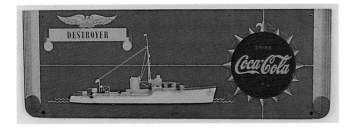

Masonite and wood destroyer ship sign, 1940s, EX, $200.00. Mitchell Collection

Masonite, horizontal, "Drink Coca-Cola Fountain Service," fountain heads on outside of lettering, 1930–40s, 27"x14", EX, $1,200.00. Gary Metz

Masonite, Sprite Boy in arrow through cooler, 1940s, EX, $700.00. Mitchell Collection

Masonite, die cut, pretty blond girl holding a glass and a bouquet of flowers, 1940s, 42"x40", VG, $450.00. Gary Metz

Metal and plastic light-up counter sign, waterfall motion, "Pause and Refresh," 1950s, EX, $1,150.00. Gary Metz

Masonite, "Drink," featuring bottle, 1940s, 54"x19", EX $475.00

Masonite, oval, "Drink Coca-Cola," white lettering on red, 1940, 13"x5½", EX $200.00

Masonite with metal arrow, 1940s, 17", EX $800.00

Metal and glass light-up, motion, red "Drink Coca-Cola" button in center with motion appearance between button and gold case, 1960s, 11¼" dia, VG $375.00

Metal bag holder, painted, "For Home Refreshment Coca-Cola," Sprite Boy, 36"x17", VG, $400.00.

Metal, "Drink Coca-Cola, Delicious and Refreshing," bottle on left side, "The Icy-O Company Inc, Charlotte, N.C.," EX, $850.00. Gary Metz

Metal, "Drink Coca-Cola in Bottles," original bent wire frame and stand, white lettering on red background wire is painted white, 1950s, EX, $160.00. Gary Metz

Metal, double sided, "In any weather Drink Coca-Cola," thermometer on one side fits on outside of screen door, while the "Thanks, Call Again" fits on the inside of the door, rare, 1930s, $2,100.00. Gary Metz

Metal, building, "Drink Coca-Cola," 1950–60s, 48" dia, EX $175.00

Metal button, 12", with wings, Sprite Boy on ends and lettering of Sundaes and Malts in between, 1950s, 12"x78", VG $1,050.00

Metal fishtail, painted, "Coca-Cola Sign of Good Taste," bottle on right side of sign, 31¾"x11¾", G, $175.00.

Metal, "Drink Coca-Cola Ice Cold," original four type bracket, 1930s, NM $500.00

Metal fishtail, painted horizontal, "Coca-Cola, Sign of Good Taste," white lettering on red background on white frame with green stripes, 1960s, 46"x16", EX, $185.00.

Metal golf hole, 1950s, EX, $265.00. Mitchell Collection

Metal, horizontal, "Drink Coca-Cola," Sprite Boy in spot light, red background outlined in yellow with white lettering, 57"x18", VG, $450.00.

Metal, horizontal, painted, "Enjoy Coca-Cola," red background with white lettering and a white background block on right side with bottle centered in box, 1960, 32"x11¾", $110.00.

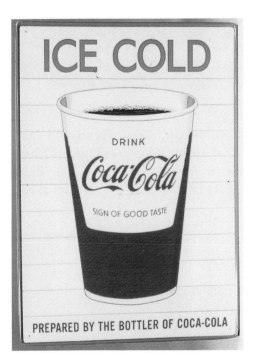

Metal, "Ice cold" with cup in center, 1960s, 20"x28", NM, $275.00. Gary Metz

Metal lollipop, "Drink Coca-Cola Refresh!," not on proper base, 1950s, $495.00. Riverview Antique Mall

Metal fountain service, 1936, 27"x14", EX $400.00

Metal light-up, "Drink Coca-Cola" on disc, wall basket, 1950s, EX. $275.00

Metal rack, round, "Take home a Carton," 1930–40s, EX, $200.00. Gary Metz

Metal, "Pause Refresh yourself," various scenes in yellow border, lettering, 1950s, 28"x10", VG, $200.00.
Mitchell Collection

Metal, sidewalk, "For Headache and Exhaustion Drink Coca-Cola," with 4" legs, manufactured by Ronemers & Co, Baltimore, M.D, 1895–90, G, $7,500.00. Gary Metz

Metal policeman crossing guard with original base. This is a very volatile piece, I've seen them sell for as little as $600.00 or as high as $3,500.00, 1950s, G, $1,100.00. Goodletsville Antique Mall

Metal, "Serve Coke at Home," 16" button at top, 1948, EX, $575.00. Gary Metz

Metal string holder with double sided panels, "Take Home Coca-Cola in Cartons," featured with six pack for 25¢, 1930s, EX, $1,100.00.
Gary Metz

Metal pilaster, bottle under a 16" "Drink Coca-Cola" button, 1950, EX $325.00

Metal pilaster, six pack being sold with a 16" "Sign of good taste" button on top, 1947, NM $550.00

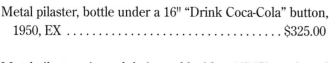

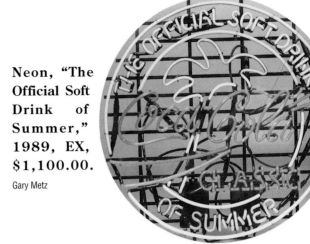

Neon, "The Official Soft Drink of Summer," 1989, EX, $1,100.00. Gary Metz

Metal whirly top with original base with four wings and eight sides for advertisement, NOS, 1950, NM, $750.00. Gary Metz

Neon, "Coca-Cola in bottles," great colors with metal base, 1950s, EX, $1,200.00. Gary Metz

Neon, "Coke with Ice," three colors, 1980s, EX, $350.00. Gary Metz

Metal policeman, unusual paint on shield that reads "Stop Emergency Vehicles Only," 1957, 5" tall, EX . . . $1,400.00

Metal sidewalk, "Coca-Cola Ice Cold Sold Here," for curb service, 1931, 20"x28", VG $175.00

Metal sidewalk fishtail, "Ice Cold," 1960s, NM $170.00

Metal sidewalk with case of drinks, 1957, EX. $200.00

Mobile, red disc, double sided, 1950s, 19" $600.00

Neon, "Coca-Cola," dynamic wave logo, M. $600.00

Neon, "Coca-Cola In Bottles," on original base, rare, 1930–1940, EX $4,200.00

Neon counter top, "Drink Coca-Cola in Bottles" on a wrinkle paint base with rubber feet on bottom, 1939, 17"x13½", VG $1,700.00

Neon disc, "Drink...Sign of Good Taste," 1950s, 16" dia, EX. $500.00

Neon, "Enjoy Coca-Cola," two-color red and white, NOS, M $350.00

Paper, bottler's calendar advance print, Garden Girl on a golf course, framed under glass, rare, 1919, NM, $7,500.00. Mitchell Collection

Oil cloth, Lillian Nordica, "Coca-Cola at Soda Fountain 5¢" Delicious Refreshing," rare, 1904, 25"x47", EX, $10,000.00.

Neon, girl drinking from a can, pink, red, and yellow, in original box, new, 20"x20", EX $180.00

Neon window unit, "Drink Coca-Cola," two colors, 1940s, 28"x18", EX. $600.00

Oil painting by Hayden Hayden, original, rosy cheeked woman holding a glass, framed, 1940s, 24"x28", EX $4,000.00

Oil painting, girl with mittens holding a glass, 1940, 24"x28", Hayden, NM $4,500.00

Paper advertising, "See adventures of Kit Carson," 1953, 24"x16", EX, $85.00. The Mitchell Collection

Oval, string hung, "Drink Coca-Cola Evegerkuhlt," German, 1930s, 12½"x8¼", EX. $45.00

Paper, Autumn Girl, in original wood frame, 1941, 16"x27", VG $750.00

Paper, bell-shaped glass with logo at top, in original black frame, 1930, 6"x9½", EX. $2,000.00

Paper, "Come in...we have Coca-Cola 5¢," Sprite Boy with glasses, 1944, 25"x8", VG, $300.00. Gary Metz

Paper, calendar print sent to bottlers in advance of calendar, two models on a beach outing, framed under glass, rare, 1917, NM, $7,500.00. Mitchell Collection

Paper, "Drink Coca-Cola Delicious and Refreshing," bottle on front of hot dog, framed and under glass, EX, $150.00. Mitchell Collection

Paper, "Drink Coca-Cola, Quick Refreshment," bottle in front of hot dog, framed under glass, EX, $150.00. Mitchell Collection

Paper calendar print sent to Coca-Cola bottlers a year in advance of the calendar, Autumn Girl, rare, framed under glass, 1921, NM, $7,500.00. Mitchell Collection

Paper, Edgar Bergen and Charlie McCarthy, CBS Sunday Evenings, 1949, 22"x11", EX, $165.00. Mitchell Collection

Paper, Gibson Girl, matted and framed, if in mint condition price would go to about $4,000.00, 1910, 20"x30", F, $2,500.00. Mitchell Collection

Paper, girl in white dress with large red bow in back with a bottle and a straw, matted and framed under glass. There are two versions of this, the other one is identical except the waist bow is pink, 1910s, F, $2,500.00. Mitchell Collection

Paper, instruction for hand in bottle outdoor painted signs, framed and matted, EX, $100.00. Gary Metz

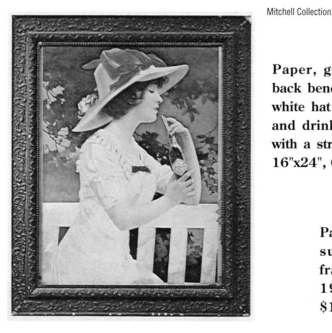

Paper, girl sitting on slat back bench wearing a large white hat with a red ribbon and drinking from a bottle with a straw, framed, 1913, 16"x24", G, $4,000.00.

Paper, Lupe Valez in swim suit holding a bottle, framed and under glass, 1932, 11"x21½", NM, $1,200.00. Mitchell Collection

Paper, "Cold" with bottle and button logo on iceberg, 1930s, EX $575.00

Paper, "Home Refreshment," three pieces of products, 1940s, NM $175.00

Paper, horizontal, "Cold Drink Coca-Cola," framed under glass, 1939, 58"x20", VG $600.00

Paper, Hilda Clark, oval "Drink Coca-Cola 5¢" sign on table, framed under glass, 1901, EX, $7,000.00.

Paper poster, horizontal, "Let's have a Coke," couple in uniform, 1930s, 57"x20", G, $850.00. Gary Metz

Paper poster, horizontal, "Such a friendly custom," two women in uniform at soda fountain, 1930s, G, $350.00. Gary Metz

Paper poster, "Ritz Boy," first time Ritz Boy was used, framed under glass, 1920s, F, $500.00. Mitchell Collection

Paper poster, "Sold Everywhere 5¢," has been trimmed, but is a rare piece, 1908, 14"x22", F, $1,050.00. Gary Metz

Paper poster, vertical, "Drink Coca-Cola Delicious and Refreshing," matted, framed under glass, 1927–28, 12"x20", VG, $475.00. Gary Metz

Paper, "Let Us Put A Case In Your Car," with red carpet, 36"x20", EX................................$230.00

Paper, "Plastic Cooler For Picnics & Parties," 1950s, NM.......................................$35.00

Paper, Sprite Boy, "Come In Have a Coke," framed under glass, EX, $150.00. Mitchell Collection

Paper poster, vertical, "Pause a minute Refresh yourself," roll down with top and bottom metal strips, 1927–28, 12"x20", EX, $1,800.00.
Gary Metz

Paper "That taste-good feeling," boy with Coca-Cola and hot dog, 1920s, EX, $650.00. Gary Metz

Paper, "which" Coca-Cola or Goldelle Ginger Ale, this one has been trimmed with lettering eliminated, framed and under glass, if mint value would increase to $7,500.00, 1905, G, $3,000.00. Mitchell Collection

Paper, two women drinking from bottles sitting in front of an ocean scene with clouds in the sky, 1912, 16"x22", VG, $4,000.00.

Paper poster, man and woman with flare glasses and the globe sitting, very rare, under glass, 1912, 38"x49", VG $16,500.00

Paper poster, flapper girl holding a bottle, 1927–28, 12"x20", VG. $475.00

Paper poster, "Now! King Size Too!," Sprite Boy between two six packs, 1955, 36"x20", NM $100.00

Paper, window display, die cut, glass shaped, "Drink Coca-Cola," rare, 12"x20", EX, $1,800.00. Gary Metz

Plywood, double sided, "Slow School Zone Enjoy Coca-Cola, Drive Safely," 1950–60s, EX, $950.00. Gary Metz

Paper, "Take Along Coke In 12oz Cans, Buy A Case," men by boat, 1960s, 35"x19", EX. $135.00

Paper, textured, travel exhibition promoting travel in France, matted and framed, 1970–80s, 24"x32", NM $160.00

Paper, "That Taste-Good Feeling," 1920s, 14"x20", VG . $275.00

Paper, "Treat Yourself Right, Drink Coca-Cola," 1920s, 12"x20", VG. $675.00

Paper, "We have Coca-Cola 5¢," Sprite Boy, rare, soda fountain hat on Sprite Boy, 1944, 22"x7", NM $500.00

Paper window set for bottle sales, three piece, "Home Refreshment," 1941, 31" tall $200.00

Paper window sign, "Let Us Put A Case In Your Car," case of Coca-Cola, 36"x20". $230.00

Plastic, curved barrel, "Be really refreshed Coca-Cola," 1960, 17"x8", EX. $25.00

Plastic, "Delicious With Ice Cold Coca-Cola," popcorn box overflowing with popcorn, 24"x7", EX. $35.00

Plastic, "Drink Coca-Cola" on red oval, Canadian, 1940–50s, 11"x9", NM $275.00

Plastic, "Here's the real thing. Coke," wave logo, 1970s, 51"x7", M $25.00

Porcelain bottle button, 3' dia, M. $550.00

Porcelain, bottle button with "Coca-Cola" across bottle front, 24", EX $450.00

Porcelain bottle, die cut, 16" tall, NM $275.00

Porcelain bottle, die cut, 1950s, 16", EX $250.00

Porcelain bottle, die cut, 1940s, 12", VG $100.00

Porcelain button, candy, film with Coke in center, 1950, 18"x30", NM $275.00

Porcelain button, NOS, 1940s, 24", M. $800.00

Porcelain, "Come In! Have A Coca-Cola," yellow and white, 1940s, 54", NM $1,100.00

Porcelain double-sided lunch sign, 1950s, 28"x25", NM, $1,500.00. Gary Metz

Porcelain, "Drink Coke," "Ask for it either way," 1940s, 9" dia, EX, $350.00. Mitchell Collection

Porcelain, double sided, "Drink Coca-Cola" with bottle in yellow circle at bottom of sign, 1939, 5'x4', G $300.00

Porcelain, double-sided flange, "Coca-Cola Here," colorful in yellow, red, and white, Canadian, 1952, 18"x20", VG $190.00

Porcelain, "Drink Coca-Cola Delicious & Refreshing," 1930s, EX $500.00

Porcelain, "Drink Coca-Cola Delicious & Refreshing," self framing, 1930s, 4'x8', NM $700.00

Porcelain, "Drink Coca-Cola, Ice Cold," fountain dispenser, 1950s, 28"x28", EX $500.00

Porcelain, "Drink Coca-Cola" on button over bottle, 1950s, 18"x28", NM $500.00

Porcelain, "Drink Coca-Cola" on fishtail, 1950–60s, 44"x16", NM $275.00

Porcelain, "Drink Coca-Cola," trademark in C tail, white lettering on red background, 1910–20s, 30"x12", VG $575.00

Porcelain, "Drug Store" over "Drink Coca-Cola Delicious & Refreshing," red, white, and green, 1930s, 90"x60", EX. $625.00

Porcelain flange, die cut, "Rafraîchissez vous Coca-Cola," foreign, VG, $400.00.

Porcelain cooler, die cut, white with black trim, 1930s, 18", EX $700.00

Porcelain, "Delicious & Refreshing," white background, 1950s, 24"x24", EX $275.00

Porcelain delivery truck cab, "Ice Cold," red, white, and yellow, arched top, 1930s, NM $700.00

Porcelain, double sided, "Drink Coca-Cola" on one side, "Isenhower Cigar Store" on other side, 1930, 30"x40", G. $200.00

Porcelain, horizontal, "Drink Coca-Cola Fountain Service," yellow background, 1950s, 28"x12", $700.00. Gary Metz

Porcelain, horizontal, "Coca-Cola Sold Here Ice Cold," red background trimmed in yellow with white lettering, 1940s, 29"x12", G, $90.00.

Porcelain, featuring hand pulling dispenser top, 1930, 24"x26", EX................................$450.00

Porcelain flange, double sided, "Refresh yourself! Coca-Cola Sold Here, Ice Cold," 1930s, EX...........$800.00

Porcelain flange, "Enjoy Coca-Cola In bottles," very rare and hard to find, 1948, EX....................$850.00

Porcelain, flange mount, "Iced Coca-Cola Here," yellow and white lettering on red background with yellow trim around outside of sign, 1950s, NM............$500.00

Porcelain, fountain service, diagonal, "Drink Coca-Cola," 1933, 22"x26", NM.......................$1,100.00

Porcelain, fountain service, double sided, red and white fountain head and glass, 1950s, 28"x28", NM..$1,600.00

Porcelain fountain service, "Drink Coca-Cola Fountain Service," white and yellow lettering on red and black background framed by fountain heads, 27"x14", EX. $1,200.00

Porcelain, "Fountain Service, Drink Coca-Cola" on button, 1950s, 34"x12", NM.........................$400.00

Porcelain fountain service, green lettering on white background with red decoration and "Drink Coca-Cola" in red bull's eye at right, 1950s, 30"x12", EX..........$300.00

Porcelain fountain service, two sided, dispenser with stainless steel banding around the edge of the sign, 1950s, 27"x28", VG................................$275.00

Porcelain outdoor, "Drink Coca-Cola Delicious and Refreshing," white and yellow lettering on red background, 1938, 8'x4', NM....................$1,300.00

Porcelain outdoor bottle, tall vertical, "Drink Coca-Cola," believed to be a foreign sign where English was the dominant language, 1950–60s, 16"x4', NM, $550.00. Gary Metz

Porcelain outdoor, "Drink Coca-Cola, Delicious and Refreshing," white lettering on red background, 1932, 5'x3', G......................................$450.00

Porcelain, sidewalk, double sided, courtesy panel over a 24" button, NOS, 1950s, 2'x5', EX...........$3,200.00

Porcelain, sidewalk, double sided, "Drink Coca-Cola In Bottles," 1940–50s, 4'x4½', VG..................$425.00

Reverse glass, "Drink Coca-Cola," 1920s, 10"x6", EX, $1,200.00.

Porcelain sidewalk, double sided vertical, "Stop Here Drink Coca-Cola," Canadian, 1941, 26"x36", EX, $325.00. Gary Metz

Reverse glass, "Drink Coca-Cola," metal frame that could be illuminated from the back, 1930s, 13"x9", F, $600.00. Mitchell Collection

Reverse glass, "Drink Coca-Cola," for back bar mirror, 1930s, 11" dia, EX, $525.00.
Mitchell Collection

Stainless steel from dispenser, "Drink Coca-Cola," horizontal lettering, 1930s, 6½"x3¼", $75.00. Gary Metz

Porcelain, truck cab, "Drink Coca-Cola in Bottles," red lettering on white background, 1950, EX $200.00

Porcelain truck cab, "Drink Coca-Cola Ice Cold," yellow and white lettering on red background trimmed in yellow, 1950s, G $375.00

Porcelain wall, one sided, advertising fountain service, red and green background with yellow and white lettering, 1934, G $650.00

Tin bottle, embossed, 1931, 4½"x12½", VG, $375.00. Gary Metz

Tin, bottle, Christmas, 1933, 3' tall, EX, $1,000.00.

Tin, bottle, die cut embossed, 3' tall, VG, $350.00. Gary Metz

Reverse glass light-up, "Drink Coca-Cola In Bottles," by Cincinnati Advertising Products Co, rare, 1920s, 15"x7"x5", EX $2,000.00

Reverse glass mirror, "Please Pay when Served, Drink Coca-Cola, Thank You," 1920–1930, 11¼" dia, EX. $250.00

Rice paper napkin with girl and bottle with arrow, framed and matted under glass, EX $50.00

Rice paper napkin with Oriental scene, VG $350.00

"Sign of Good Taste," ribbon attachments on both streamers, 1957, 3'x4', NM $100.00

Tin arrow, "Ice Cold Coca-Cola Sold Here," white lettering on red and green background, 30", G $200.00

Tin bottle, die cut, 1951, 3' tall, EX $250.00

Tin, bottle, oval, "Drink A Bottle of Carbonated Coca-Cola," rare, 1900s, 8½"x10½", EX, $7,500.00.

Tin bottle, die cut, 1954, 20"x6', NM $575.00

Tin bottle, die cut embossed, from a larger sign, 38" tall, EX $275.00

Tin button, white painted with bottle in center, 1940s, 24" dia, NM, $400.00. Gary Metz

Tin, button, with mechanic on duty under the button, 1950–60s, VG, $465.00. Riverview Antique Mall

Tin distributors, oval, from Me Rae Coca-Cola Bottling Co. in Helena, GA, featuring pretty long-haired girl, 1910, EX, $3,000.00.

Tin bottle, die-cut, 1956, 16", NM $300.00

Tin, bottle, embossed die cut, with original silver and black wooden frame, 2'x4', NM $475.00

Tin, bottle in original frame, on white background, 1950s, 36"x18", EX $200.00

Tin, bottle rack, double sided, round, "Take Home a Carton," yellow and white lettering on red background, 1930–1940, EX $240.00

Tin, bottle, vertical, in original silver wood frame, full-color bottle on white background, 1950s, 1½'x3', EX . . $225.00

Tin button, "Drink Coca-Cola Sign of Good Taste," yellow and white lettering, 1950s, 16", NM $375.00

Tin button, showing bottle on white, 1940–1950, 24", EX $275.00

Tin button with arrow, red lettering on white, all original hardware, 1950s, 16" dia, EX $500.00

Tin, "Candy-Cigarettes" over fishtail logo, self-framed, 1960s, 28"x20", EX $225.00

Tin, "Coca-Cola," red background with green and yellow border, bottle centered, 1930s, 45" dia, EX $375.00

Tin, "Cold Drinks," 1960s, 24"x15", NM $200.00

Tin, "Cold Drinks" with "Drink" fishtail, "With Crushed Ice," 1960s, 24"x15", NM $225.00

Tin, "Drink Coca-Cola," 24" iron frame, one side has a 16" button while the opposite side as a 10" plastic button with a small light which creates a back light, VG, $975.00. Gary Metz

Tin, double sided die-cut arrow flange, "Drink Coca-Cola Ice Cold," with button at top and bottle in lower arrow point, EX, $400.00. Gary Metz

Tin, "Drink Coca-Cola" button with silver metal arrow, 1950–60s, 18" dia., $700.00. Mitchell Collection

Tin, "Drink Coca-Cola Enjoy that Refreshing New Feeling," self-framed, painted, fishtail design, 1960s, 28"x12", VG, $180.00. Gary Metz

Tin, Dasco bottle with 1923 bottle, 1931, 4½"x12", M. $625.00

Tin, "Deli" with "Drink Coca-Cola" on dot at right, 1950s, 50"x15", NM $425.00

Tin, diamond shaped, with bottle spotlighted at bottom, in original black wooden frame, "Drink Coca-Cola" at top, 1940, 42"x42", NM $500.00

Tin, die cut, double sided, "Drink & Take Home A Carton," 1930s, 10"x13", EX $200.00

Tin, die-cut, two-sided hanger, 1930s, 60"x48", EX . $275.00

Tin, "Drink..." button with wings, 1950s, 32"x12", NM . $275.00

Tin, "Drink Coca-Cola Enjoy that Refreshing New Feeling," painted fishtail with Coca-Cola bottle on right side, 1960s, 32x12, VG, $150.00. Gary Metz

Tin, "Drink Coca-Cola 5¢ Ice Cold," self framing, tilted bottle, 1930s, 54"x18", EX. $350.00

Tin, "Drink Delicious Refreshing Coca-Cola," Hilda Clark, very rare, 1900, 20"x28", EX, $14,000.00.

Tin, "Drink Coca-Cola 5¢ Ice Cold," white and yellow lettering on red background with vertical bottle in yellow bull's eye, 1938, NM $350.00

Tin, "Drink Coca-Cola," American Artworks with scalloped top and filigree, 1936, EX $850.00

Tin, "Drink Coca-Cola," bottle at right, self framing, 1951, 28"x10", EX. $160.00

Tin, "Drink Coca-Cola" button next to bottle, green border, 1950s, 28"x20", EX $400.00

Tin, "Drink Coca-Cola Delicious & Refreshing," couple with a bottle, 1940s, 28"x20", EX $550.00

Tin, "Drink Coca-Cola Delicious & Refreshing," couple with bottle, self-framing, 1940s, NM $775.00

Tin, "Drink Coca-Cola" fishtail, "Refreshes You Best," self-framing, 1960s, 28"x20", EX $200.00

Tin, "Drink Coca-Cola" fishtail, white lettering on red fishtail against white sign background, 7½"x3½", NM. $20.00

Tin, "Drink Coca-Cola Fountain Service," red, green, and white lettering on yellow, red, and white background, 1950s, 28"x12", NM $575.00

Tin, "Drink Coca-Cola Ice Cold" on red disc with bars, 1930s, 28"x20", EX. $250.00

Tin, "Drink Coca-Cola Ice-Cold" over "Delicious & Refreshing" on bottles with green background, 1940s, 28"x20", EX $175.00

Tin "Drink Coca-Cola in Bottles" button, all white lettering, 1955, 12", NM. $270.00

Tin "Drink Coca-Cola In Bottles" button with arrow shooting from right to left at about 2 and 8 o'clock, 1954, EX $325.00

Tin, "Drink Coca-Cola" in left and center with yellow dot bottle at lower right, 1940s, 28"x20", EX $325.00

Tin, "Drink Coca-Cola" lettered in white over dynamic wave logo, 1980s, 24"x18", EX $40.00

Tin, "Drink Coca-Cola," marching bottles to left side of sign, 1937, 54"x18", EX $800.00

Tin, "Drink Coca-Cola" over yellow dot bottle, "5¢ Ice Cold" below, self framing, 1940s, 54"x18", EX. $600.00

Tin, "Drink Coca-Cola," red background with yellow and white lettering featuring three receding bottles, 1930s, 54"x18", EX. $750.00

Tin, "Drink Coca-Cola Sign of Good Taste," white and yellow lettering, 1950s, 24", EX $425.00

Tin, "Drink Coca-Cola," white on red with bottle at right on white background, self framing, 1956, NM. $150.00

Tin, "Drink Coca-Cola," with smiling girl, self framing, 1940s, 28"x20", NM $450.00

Tin, "Drink" over bottle, "Coca-Cola" under bottle, 1930s, 5"x13", EX. $300.00

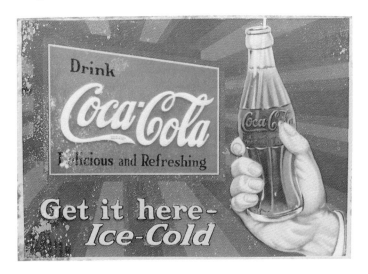

Tin, embossed over cardboard with string holder, "Drink Coca-Cola," 1922, 8"x4", EX, $900.00. Gary Metz

Tin, embossed, "Drink Coca-Cola Delicious and Refreshing," 14"x10", F, $210.00. Gary Metz

Tin, embossed, painted, foreign, 17¼"x53", G, $100.00.

Tin, featuring Elaine holding a glass, 1916, 20"x30", VG, $5,000.00.

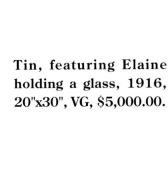

Tin, "Drink," white on red with silver frame, 1950s, 34"x18", EX. $155.00

Tin, embossed, "Drink Coca-Cola," 1920, 18"x5¾", VG. $475.00

Tin, embossed, "Drink Coca-Cola in Bottles 5¢," 1920, 23"x6", EX. $450.00

Tin, embossed, "Drink Coca-Cola" lettered in white on red with green border, 1920s, NM $825.00

Tin, embossed, "Ice Cold Coca-Cola Sold Here," 1923 bottle inset at left, 1931, 28"x20", M $950.00

Tin, embossed, "Ice Cold Coca-Cola Sold Here," green and white trim, 1933, 19½" dia, EX $475.00

Tin, "Enjoy Coca-Cola All the Year Round," with giant earth, 1982, 33"x24", EX $110.00

Tin, Hilda Clark, round, "Coca-Cola Drink Delicious and Refreshing," very rare and hard to find piece, 1903, 6" dia, EX, $5,000.00.

Tin, Hilda Clark, considered rare due to the fact this art work is rarely found in the tin version, 1903, 16¼"x19½", EX, $3,700.00. Gary Metz

Tin, "Enjoy that Refreshing New Feeling," fishtail logo with rolled frame, 1960s, 54"x18", NM $300.00

Tin, "Enjoy That Refreshing New Feeling" on fishtail, self-framing, 1960s, 32"x12", NM $155.00

Tin fishtail, Coca-Cola fishtail in center with bottle at right hand, red, green, and white, vertical, 1960s, 56"x32", NM $225.00

Tin, fishtail die-cut, 1960s, 12"x26", EX $250.00

Tin fishtail, "Enjoy that Refreshing New Feeling," bottle to right of fishtail, 1964, 28"x20", NM $180.00

Tin fishtail flange, "Enjoy that Refreshing New Feeling," 1962, 18"x15", EX $230.00

Tin, fishtail horizontal, "Cold Drinks Drink Coca-Cola," with crushed ice, 1960, 24"x15", NM $200.00

Tin fishtail, horizontal, "Sign of the Good Taste," full-color bottle at right side of sign, all on white background with green trim on frame, 1959, 54"x18", NM $250.00

Tin fishtail, horizontal, with bottle on right sign with "Ice Cold" beside bottle, 1958, 54"x18" $240.00

Tin fishtail, self-framed with bottle on right, "Drink Coca-Cola Enjoy that Refreshing new Feeling," horizontal, 1960s, 32"x12", NM $210.00

Tin fishtail, vertical, "Drink Coca-Cola" with bottle at bottom of sign, 1960, 18"x54", NM $230.00

Tin, flange, "Drink Coca-Cola," 1941, 24"x21", EX . . $450.00

Tin flange, "Drink Coca-Cola, Ice Cold," flange forms arrow point, 1956, 18"x22", M $475.00

Tin flat , "Refresh Yourself," 1927, 29"x28", VG $350.00

Tin, "Gas & Oil" on bottle side of fishtail logo, self framing, 1960s, 96"x16", NM $450.00

Tin, girl with glass, gold beveled edge, 1920s, 8"x11", EX . . $875.00

Tin, "Grocery" over bottle with fishtail logo, 1960s, 28"x20", G $100.00

Tin, "Have a Coke," showing a spotlighted bottle in center with "Coca-Cola" at bottom all on red background, vertical, 1948, 18"x54", EX $350.00

Tin, "Have a Coke," tilted bottle on yellow dot, 1940s, 54"x18", EX $375.00

Tin, heavy embossed,1923 bottle at each end, "Drink Coca-Cola" in center in white on red background, 1930s, EX $425.00

Tin, horizontal, "Drink Coca-Cola," red background, silver border on self frame with bottle in spotlight in lower right hand corner, 1946, 28"x20", EX, $340.00. Gary Metz

Tin, horizontal, "Drink Coca-Cola," self-framing, white, VG, 32"x10½", 1927, $725.00. Gary Metz

Tin, Hilda Clark, showing her drinking from a glass while seated at a table with roses and stationary, very rare, 1899, VG, $15,000.00.

Tin, horizontal embossed, "Drink Coca-Cola Ice Cold," framed and matted white and yellow lettering on red and black background, bottle in left part of sign, 1936, 28"x20", EX, $800.00. Gary Metz

Tin, horizontal, "Drink Coca-Cola Ice Cold," with bottle at right, red and white, 1957, 28"x20", EX......... $150.00

Tin, horizontal embossed, "Drink Coca-Cola," 1923 bottle on left side, 35"x12", EX, $350.00. Gary Metz

Tin, horizontal, "Drink Coca-Cola In Bottles," 1916 bottle at left of sign, 1920s, 35"x12", G $150.00

Tin, horizontal, "Things go better with Coke," self framing, 1960s, 32"x12", NM $180.00

Tin, horizontal, "Things go better with Coke," self framing with full-color bottle on right, all on white background, 1960s, 54"x18", EX $200.00

Tin, Lillian Nordica, self framed, embossed, promoting both fountain and bottle sales, 1904–05, EX, $7,000.00.

Gary Metz

Tin, "Ice Cold Drinks," disc logo and cup, "Serve Yourself," 1960s, 27"x22", NM $225.00

Tin, "Ice Cold Drinks Enjoy Coca-Cola," with cup of Coke and snow flakes, 1960, 27"x22", NM $250.00

Tin, "It's A Natural! Coca-Cola In Bottles," over bottle on red background, 1950s, 16" dia, EX $375.00

Tin, "Let us put a Coke in your car," EX $100.00

Tin, octagonal, "Drink Coca-Cola" over bottle in circle, 1930s, 10" dia, EX $500.00

Tin, oval, with French lettering "Buvez Coca-Cola Glace," Canadian, 1950s, 3'x2', EX $210.00

Tin, Lillian Nordica, oval framed, "Coca-Cola Delicious and Refreshing," featuring Coca-Cola table and oval "Drink Coca-Cola 5¢," rare, 1904, 8¾"x10¼", EX, $7,500.00.

Tin, Lillian Nordica, oval framed with framed back drop showing "Delicious and Refreshing 5¢," 1905, 8¼"x10¼", EX, $7,000.00.

Tin over cardboard, "Treat Yourself To A Coke," 1950–60s, EX $140.00

Tin, painted, "Coca-Cola," made in U.S.A/AAW 10-37, red background with white lettering and bottle in center outlined in green, 1934, 45" dia, $400.00.

Tin, painted, "Drink Coca-Cola in Bottles 5¢," horizontally lettered, if this sign were EX to M price would increase to the $1,000.00 – $1,200.00 range, 1900s, 34½"x11¾", F, $375.00.

Tin, painted, "Drink Coca-Cola," shoulders and head of girl drinking from a bottle, yellow and white lettering on red background, self framing, 1940, 34"x12", EX, $425.00. Gary Metz

Tin, painted, "Take a case home today $1.00 deposit," 19½"x27¾", VG, $100.00.

Tin, painted litho, "Drink Coca-Cola In Bottles 5¢," bottle on each side, framed, 1907, 34½"x12", F, $400.00.

Tin "Pause...Drink Coca-Cola," considered to be rare due to the 1939 – 40 cooler in the left-hand spotlight, all on red background horizontal lettering, self framing, 1940, 42'x18', EX, $2,400.00. Gary Metz

Tin, "Pause Drink Coca-Cola" on bottle in yellow center dot, 1940s, 54"x18", EX $175.00

Tin, "Pause, Drink Coca-Cola," tilted bottle on yellow dot, self framing, 1930s, 54"x18", EX. $225.00

Tin, "Pause Drink Coca-Cola," white lettering on red and yellow background, vertical, 1930s, 18"x54", EX . $220.00

Tin sidewalk, embossed, "French Wine Coca," with 9" legs, close up of center inset (right), 1885–88, 27¾"x 19¾", VG, $7,500.00.
Gary Metz

Tin, sidewalk, embossed, "Take home a carton," 1942, 20"x28", EX, $375.00. Gary Metz

Tin, self framing, horizontal oval, "Coca-Cola," girl in foreground of lettering offering a bottle, 1926, 11"x8", F, $200.00. Gary Metz

Tin, painted vertical, "Serve Coca-Cola at home," yellow and white lettering on red background with a six pack spotlighted in the center, 1951, 18"x54", EX, $300.00. Gary Metz

Tin, rectangular, man and woman with a bottle, "Drink Coca-Cola Delicious & Refreshing," all on red background, 1941, 28"x20", NM. $850.00

Tin, "Refresh Yourself, Drink Coca-Cola, Sold Here Ice Cold," 1927, 29"x30", G $150.00

Tin, self framing rectangle, "Coca-Cola," oval inside rectangle framing girl presenting a bottle, 1926, 11"x8½", EX, $2,000.00.

Tin six pack, embossed die cut, 1963, 3'x2½', EX, $725.00. Gary Metz

Tin six pack, embossed die cut, featuring a King Size six pack, 1963, 3'x2½', EX, $700.00. Gary Metz

Tin, "Refresh Yourself Drink Coca-Cola Sold Here Ice Cold," trimmed in red and green, 1920s, 28"x29", EX $375.00

Tin, ribbon, die cut, "Sign of Good Taste," 1957, 3', NM . $210.00

Tin, "Serve Coca-Cola at home," six pack highlighted at center of sign all on red background, vertical, 1950, 18"x54", EX $450.00

Tin, "Serve Coca-Cola At Home," yellow dot six pack, 1950s, 54"x18", NM $250.00

Tin sidewalk sign, big King Size, fishtail design with bottle, 1958–1960, 20"x28", EX $120.00

Tin, "Sign of Good Taste," fishtail logo, with raised border, 1960s, 32"x11", EX $175.00

Tin, "Sign of Good Taste, Ice Cold," fishtail logo and bottle, 1960s, 56"x32", EX $175.00

Tin, "Sign of Good Taste," vertical fishtail, green rolled frame, 1960s, 18"x54", NM $250.00

Tin, six pack, die cut, "6 for 25¢," 1950s, EX $500.00

Tin, "Take Home a carton," self framing border, Canadian, 1950, 35x53, $625.00. Gary Metz

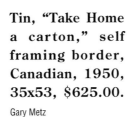

Tin, six pack, die cut, "King Size, Coca-Cola," 1960s, EX $300.00

Tin, six-pack, die-cut, red wire handle, 1950s, EX . . $375.00

Tin, "Take A Case Home Today, Quality Refreshment," red carpet with a yellow Coke case on it, 1950s, 28"x20", NM $325.00

Tin, "Take a case home today," white and yellow lettering on red background, vertical, 1949, 20"x28", NM . $220.00

Tin, "Take Home A Carton," fishtail green border, 1960s, 28"x20", EX $225.00

Tin, "Take Home A Carton" over six pack, Canadian, 1950s, 53"x35", NM $575.00

Tin, "Things Go Better With Coke" left of bottle, raised border, 1960s, 24"x24", EX $200.00

Tin, "Things Go Better With Coke" on right, with disc logo at left, 1960s, 21"x11", EX $250.00

Tin, "Things Go Better With Coke," red border, 1960s, 32"x12", EX $175.00

Tin, "Things Go Better With Coke" with bottle, disc logo on both sides raised border, 1960s, 54"x18", EX . $225.00

Tin, twelve pack, die cut, 1954, 20"x13", NM $550.00

Tin, vertical, "Drink Delicious Refreshing Coca-Cola," Hilda Clark, one of the oldest signs known to exist, and the first celebrity to endorse the product, lettering under pen reads "Coca-Cola makes flow of thought more easy and reasoning power more vigorous," 1899, 20"x28", VG, $10,500.00. Gary Metz

Tin, vertical painted,"Drink Coca-Cola Ice-Cold Delicious and Refreshing," green background with button at top and yellow lettering beneath button, 1941, G, $200.00.

Tin, two-sided die-cut triangle with hanging bracket, "Drink Coca-Cola" at top, white lettering on red background with "Ice Cold" at bottom over bottle, 1937, G $575.00

Tin two-sided flange, "Ice Cold Coca-Cola Sold Here," white lettering on red and green background, 1920s, 12½"x10", G $300.00

Tin two-sided flange with attached 16" buttons at top of arrow, 1950s, G. $725.00

Tin two-sided rack, "Six bottles for 25¢, Take Home a Carton," 1937, 13"x10", EX $250.00

Wire and tin, "Whatever you do," fish jumping or fishing fly, 1960, 14"x18", EX, $170.00. Gary Metz

Wire and tin, "Whatever you do," saddle on fence, 1960s, 14"x18", EX, $170.00. Gary Metz

Wire and tin, "Wherever you go," skier coming down a snow slope, 1960s, 14"x18", EX, $170.00. Gary Metz

Wire and tin, "Wherever you go," tropical island, 1960s, 14"x18", EX, $120.00. Gary Metz

Tin, vertical, "Sign of Good Taste," fishtail logo at top over bottle, 1960s, 18"x54", EX $175.00

Tin, vertical, "Take Home A Carton, Big King Size," six pack of big Cokes, self framing, 1962, 20"x28", EX $250.00

Tin, with button and bottle, Canadian, 1956, 28"x20", EX. $450.00

Window decal, "Drink Coca-Cola" with fret work top, 1940, 25"x12", M $110.00

Wood and masonite, "Beverage Department" with Sprite Boy, 1950s, NM $1,200.00

Wood and masonite, hanging, "Drink Coca-Cola. Delicious...Refreshing," with silhouette in left-hand side, 1941, 3'x1', NM. $950.00

Wood and masonite, Kay Displays industry work refreshed sign, 1940s, EX. $200.00

Wood and masonite, Kay Displays refreshed communication sign, 1940s, EX $200.00

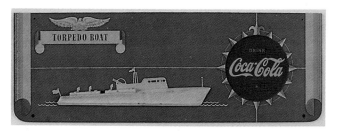

Wood and masonite, wartime torpedo boat, 1940, EX, $200.00. Mitchell Collection

Wood and plastic, "Drink Coca-Cola" in fishtail sign, 15½"x12", VG, $50.00.

Wood arrow, "Drink Coca-Cola Ice Cold," silver painted bottle and arrow, 17" dia, F, $400.00. Gary Metz

Wood, figural, die cut, "Coca-Cola" cooler, probably part of another sign, 1950s, EX, $260.00. Gary Metz

Wood and masonite, Kay Displays work refreshed, science, 1940, EX $200.00

Wood and masonite, work refreshed, highlighting education, 1940, EX $200.00

Wood and plastic, "Drink Coca-Cola," advertising bar for Roden Soda Bar, unusual Canadian piece, 1940–1950s, 11"x9", NM $260.00

Wood bottle, 3-D, silver bottle, red background, 1940s, 2'x4', EX. $250.00

Wood, "Here's Refreshment," bottle and horseshoe on plank, 1940s, EX, $325.00. Mitchell Collection

Wood and masonite, Kay Displays transportation, work refreshed, 1940s, EX $200.00

Wood and masonite, Kay Displays work refreshed, agriculture, 1940, EX. $200.00

Wood, "Drink Coca-Cola" above gold bottle and leaf designs, 1930s, 23"x23", EX $900.00

Wood medallion, Kay Displays, "Drink Coca-Cola," bottle with leaves at bottom, 1930s, EX, $1,300.00.

Wood, Sprite Boy Welcome Friend, 1940, 32"x14", EX, $550.00. Mitchell Collection

Wood, Silhouette Girl, metal hanger, 1940, EX, $450.00. Mitchell Collection

Wood, Kay Displays, "Drink Coca-Cola," two glasses on top of red emblem, 1930s, 9"x11", M $875.00

Wood, Kay Displays, metal at top showing glasses of Coca-Cola, 1930, EX. $900.00

Wood, Kay Displays, "Please Pay Cashier," filigree on ends, 1930s, 22"x12", EX $1,500.00

Wood, Kay Displays "Please Pay Cashier" with Coca-Cola at bottom, 22"x12½", 1950, EX $200.00

Wood, Kay Displays, "Quick Service," 1930, 3"x10", VG $2,100.00

Wood, Kay Displays, "While Shopping" with "Drink Coca-Cola" at center, 1930, 3"x10", VG $1,500.00

Wood, Kay Displays, "While Shopping" with red "Drink Coca-Cola" below, 1930s, 10"x3", EX $1,700.00

Wood, Kay Displays, "Ye Wha Enter Here" on board above emblem, 1940s, 39"x11", EX $475.00

Wood, "Please Pay Cashier," cut out rope hanger, 1950s, 15"x19", EX $200.00

Wood, "Quick Service" on board with red "Drink Coca-Cola" emblem below, 1930s, 10"x3", EX $2,000.00

Wood, "Resume Speed/Slow School Zone" two sided on diamonds, 1960s, 48", EX $875.00

Wood, "Slow School Zone," silhouette girl running, "Resume Speed" on back, 1957, 16"x48", EX $350.00

Wood, "Sundae/Malt," button logo and Sprite Boy, 1950s, 12"x78", EX $975.00

Wood, "Yes," swimming girl miniature billboard, EX . $115.00

Calendars

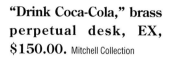

"Drink Coca-Cola," brass perpetual desk, EX, $150.00. Mitchell Collection

1891, from ASA Chandler & Co. featuring girl in period dress holding a sport racquet with full pad moved to reveal full face of sheet, rare, EX, $10,500.00.

1897, "Coca-Cola at all Soda Fountains," all monthly pads displayed at once, 7"x12", EX, $9,000.00.

1900, Hilda Clark at table with glass, all month pads displayed on front sheet, rare, 7"x12", EX, $8,500.00.

1901, "Drink Coca-Cola at all Soda Fountains 5¢" with full monthly pad, framed, matted, and under glass, rare, EX, $5,000.00.

1902, "Drink Coca-Cola 5¢" with wrong month sheet, EX, $5,000.00.

1904, Lillian Nordica standing by table with a glass, 7"x15", EX, $4,000.00.

1905, Lillian Nordica standing beside table holding fan, table has a glass, framed, matted, and under glass, 7"x15", EX, $4,500.00.

1906, Juanita, "Drink Coca-Cola Delicious Refreshing," framed, matted, under glass, 7"x15", $4,000.00.

1907, "Drink Coca-Cola Delicious Refreshing, Relieves fatigue Sold Everywhere 5¢" featuring woman in period dress holding up a glass of Coca-Cola, EX, $5,500.00.

1908, "Drink Coca-Cola Relieves Fatigue Sold Everywhere 5¢," top only, double this price if calendar is complete, 7x14, EX, $1,500.00.

1909, Lillian Nordica beside tall table with a glass, full pad, framed under glass, 3¾,"x7", EX, $950.00. Mitchell Collection

1910, the Coca-Cola Girl with partial month pad framed, matted under glass, 8"x17", King, EX, $4,500.00.

1911, the Coca-Cola Girl, "Drink Delicious Coca-Cola," framed under glass, 10"x17", Hamilton King, M, $3,200.00. Mitchell Collection

1912, "Drink Coca-Cola Delicious Refreshing," wrong calendar pad, correct pad should be at bottom of picture, King, EX, $2,000.00.

1913, "Drink Coca-Cola Delicious Refreshing," girl drinking from flare glass with syrup line, 13"x22", King, EX, $3,500.00.

1913, top, girl in white hat with red ribbon, value would double if complete, rare piece matted and framed under glass, EX, $3,000.00. Mitchell Collection

1914, Betty, top with monthly pad missing, this piece has the bottle featured which is rare, if it were intact and in G to EX condition value would increase to $5,000.00, G, $2000.00. Mitchell Collection

1914, Betty, with full pad and original metal strip at top, VG, $1,000.00. Gary Metz

1912, "Drink Coca-Cola Delicious Refreshing," large version of this year's calendar, 12"x30", King, EX . $4,500.00

1915, Elaine, matted and framed with partial pad, VG, $1,300.00. Gary Metz

1916, Elaine with glass, partial pad, under glass in frame, 13"x32", M, $1,500.00. Mitchell collection

1916, the World War I Girl holding a glass, she also appears holding a bottle of another version, wrong pad, framed, 13"x32", EX, $1,500.00.

1917, Constance, with glass, full pad, framed and matted under glass, EX, $1,800.00. Mitchell Collection

1918, June Caprice with glass, framed under glass, G, $350.00.
Mitchell Collection

1920, Garden Girl with a bottle, actually at a golf course, framed under glass, 12"x32", M, $1,700.00.

Mitchell Collection

1919, Marian Davis shown holding a glass, partial pad, framed, matted, under glass example of an early star endorsement, 6"x10½", EX, $2,500.00.

1919, the Knitting Girl, great art work of girl with bottle and a knitting bag, partial pad, framed under glass, 13"x32", EX, $2,200.00. Mitchell Collection

1923, girl with shawl and a bottle with a straw, full pad, framed under glass, 12"x24", VG, $700.00.

Mitchell Collection

1921, model sitting beside flowers with a glass, known as the Autumn Girl, partial pad, framed under glass, 12"x32", M, $1,300.00. Mitchell Collection

1922, girl at baseball game with a glass, framed under glass, 12"x32", NM, $1,800.00. Mitchell Collection

1918, two women at beach, one with a bottle, the other has a glass, wrong pad, 13"x32", EX $3,000.00

Perpetual desk showing day, month, and year, 1920, EX, $300.00.

1924, Smiling Girl in period dress holding a glass with a bottle close by, framed under glass. 12"x24", M, $900.00. Beware: Reproductions exist. Mitchell Collection

1925, Girl at Party with white fox fur and a glass, framed under glass, 12"x24", M, $900.00. Beware: Reproductions exist. Mitchell Collection

1926, girl in tennis outfit holding a glass, with a bottle, sitting by the tennis racquet, frame under glass, 10"x18", M, $1,000.00. Mitchell Collection

1927, girl in sheer dress holding a glass, with a framed bottle in foreground, partial pad, framed under glass, Taylor's Billiard Parlor, 12"x24", M, $1,750.00. Mitchell Collection

1927, "The Drink that Makes The Whole World Kin," with bottle in oval frame at lower left, framed under glass, M, $900.00. Mitchell Collection

1928, model in evening wear holding glass, partial pad, framed under glass, 12"x24", M, $850.00. Mitchell Collection

1929, girl in green dress with string of beads displaying both glass and bottle, full pad, framed under glass, 12"x24", M, $950.00. Mitchell Collection

1930, woman in swimming attire sitting on rock with canoe in foreground with bottles, display partial pad, framed under glass, 12"x24", M, $950.00. Mitchell Collection

1931, boy at fishing hole with dog, sandwich, and a bottle, full pad, framed under glass, 12"x24", Rockwell, M, $800.00. Mitchell Collection

1932, boy sitting at well with a bucket full of bottles and a dog sitting up at his feet, full pad, framed and under glass, 12"x24", Rockwell, M, $550.00. Mitchell Collection

1933, the Village Blacksmith will full pad, framed and under glass, 12"x24", Frederic Stanley, M, $750.00. Mitchell Collection

1934, girl on porch playing music for elderly gentleman with cane, full pad, framed under glass, 12"x24", Rockwell, M, $700.00. Mitchell Collection

1935, boy sitting on a stump fishing with a bottle, full pad, framed under glass, 12"x24", Rockwell, M, $550.00. Beware: Reproductions exist. Mitchell Collection

1936, 50th Anniversary, older man at small boat and a young girl enjoying a bottle, full pad, framed under glass, 12"x24", N. C. Wyeth, M, $750.00. Mitchell Collection

1937, boy walking with fishing pole over his shoulder holding a couple bottles, framed under glass, 12"x24", M, $525.00. Mitchell Collection

1938, girl sitting in front of blinds with a bottle, full pad, framed under glass, Crandall, M, $400.00.

Mitchell Collection

1939, girl starting to pour Coca-Cola from bottle into glass, unmarked, full pad, framed under glass, M, $450.00. Mitchell Collection

1940, woman in red dress with a glass and a bottle, full pad, framed and under glass, VG, $450.00. Mitchell Collection

1941, girl sitting on a log with ice skates displaying a bottle, full pad that displays two months at same time, EX, $375.00. Mitchell Collection

1942, "America Love It or Leave It" from Brownsville, TN, featuring a drum & fife attachment with monthly pads, EX, $95.00. Mitchell Collection

1942, boy and girl building snowman with a bottle, full pad displays two months at once, VG, $275.00. Mitchell Collection

1943, pocket, "Here's to our GI Joes," two girls toasting with bottles, EX, $35.00. Mitchell Collection

1943, pocket, "Tastes like Home," small, with all months shown on one front sheet, sailor drinking from a bottle, EX, $35.00. Mitchell Collection

1943, military nurse with a bottle, full pad displays two months at same time, EX, $325.00. Mitchell Collection

1945, pocket, with Sprite Boy looking around bottle on left side, EX, $40.00.

Mitchell Collection

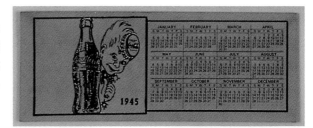

1944, woman holding a bottle, full pad, EX, $225.00.

Mitchell Collection

1945, girl in head scarf with snow falling in the background, full pad, EX, $275.00. Mitchell Collection

1946, Sprite Boy on cover with two months and a scene on each page, framed under glass, EX, $1,250.00. Mitchell Collection

1947, girl holding snow skis with mountains in background, full pad, EX, $285.00. Mitchell Collection

1948, girl in coat and gloves holding a bottle, full pad, EX, $300.00. Mitchell Collection

1949, girl in red cap with a bottle, full pad, M, $275.00. Mitchell Collection

1945, Boy Scout in front of the Scout Oath, Rockwell, M. $500.00

1946, Boy Scout den chief showing younger Cub Scout how to tie a knot, Rockwell, VG $400.00

1950, woman with a serving tray full of bottles, full pad, M, $275.00. Mitchell Collection

1951, girl at party holding a bottle, with colorful streamers in background, full pad, M, $150.00. Mitchell Collection

1952, "Coke adds Zest," party scene with a girl serving bottles from tray, full calendar pad, M, $150.00. Mitchell Collection

1953, Boy Scout, Cub Scout, and Explorer Scout in front of the Liberty Bell, Coca-Cola Bottling Works, Greenwood, Mississippi, framed and matted under glass, Rockwell, EX, $350.00. Mitchell Collection

1953, "Work Better Refreshed," work scenes with woman in center in work scarf holding a bottle, full pad, M, $150.00. Mitchell Collection

1954, "Me, too!" with 1953 Santa cover sheet, full pad, owner recorded high and low temperatures of each day, VG, $140.00. Gary Metz

1954, reference edition with full pad featuring Santa with a bottle, EX, $75.00. Mitchell Collection

1954, sports scene in background with woman in foreground holding a bottle, full calendar pad, M, $175.00. Mitchell Collection

1955, woman in hat holding a bottle, full pad, M, $175.00. Mitchell Collection

1956, famous flower paintings, reference version, EX, $20.00.

Mitchell Collection

1956, "There's nothing like a Coke," full pad, featuring girl pulling on ice skates, M, $135.00.

Mitchell Collection

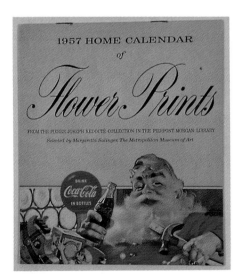

1957, reference edition of flower prints with Santa on front, M, $20.00. Mitchell Collection

1955, reference edition with Santa holding a bottle,
M $20.00

1958, reference edition with "Sign of Good Taste" with flowers against a brick background, M, $15.00. Mitchell Collection

1957, "The pause that refreshes," girl holding ski poles and a bottle, EX, $80.00. Mitchell Collection

1958, snow scene of a boy and girl with a bottle, "Sign of Good Taste," full pad, M, $175.00. Mitchell Collection

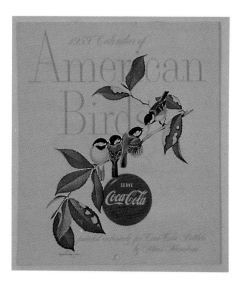

1959, birds sitting on branch with a Coke button under branch, reference version, Athos Menaboni, M, $20.00. Mitchell Collection

1959, girl being offered a bottle in front of a sports scene, full pad, G, $135.00. Mitchell Collection

1960, "Be Really Refreshed," featuring man and woman holding skis each with a bottle, full pad, M, $75.00. Mitchell Collection

1960, reference with puppies in Christmas stockings, EX, $20.00. Mitchell Collection

1961, reference with Santa sitting in an easy chair holding a glass that's being filled by an elf, M, $20.00. Mitchell Collection

1961, "Coke Refreshes You Best," woman being offered a bottle, full pad, M, $75.00. Mitchell Collection

1962, reference of birds of America, M, $20.00. Mitchell Collection

1963, reference edition with Santa Claus in middle of electric train display in front of Christmas tree with helicopter flying around his head, holding a bottle, M, $25.00. Mitchell Collection

1962, "Enjoy that Refreshing New Feeling," boy holding bottle and offering other hand to dance with a young woman, M, $75.00. Mitchell Collection

1964, reference featuring Santa standing by a fireplace with his list and a bottle, M, $20.00. The Mitchell Collection

1965, reference edition with Santa and children, M, $20.00. Mitchell Collection

**1963, "The Pause that Refreshes,"
with a woman looking at new clothes in
a door mirror, M, $75.00.** Mitchell Collection

**1964, "Things go better with
Coke," featuring a woman reclin-
ing on a couch while a man is
offering her a bottle, M, $85.00.**

Mitchell Collection

**1965, "Things go better with
Coke," a couple relaxing by a log
cabin, each with a bottle, $75.00.**

Mitchell Collection

**1966, Santa Claus standing on
ladder with a bottle and a Christmas ornament in front of a Christmas tree, M, $25.00.** Mitchell Collection

**1967, reference edition with
Santa Claus sitting at desk with a
bottle, EX, $12.00.** Mitchell Collection

**1966, man pictured holding serv-
ing tray with food and bottles over
woman's head, full pad, "Things
Go Better with Coke," M, $80.00.**

Mitchell Collection

**1967, "For the taste you never
get tired of," featuring five
women with trophy, full pad, M,
$50.00.** Mitchell Collection

1964, Japanese girl pictured on front, full pad, EX. . $375.00

1969, reference edition showing Holiday Greetings with bottle on front, M, $8.00. Mitchell Collection

1968, "Coke has the taste you never get tired of," girl looking at 45rpm record and holding a bottle, with full pad, M, $75.00. Mitchell Collection

1969, "Thing go better with Coke," featuring boy whispering into girl's ear while both are seated at a table enjoying a bottle, full pad, M, $75.00. Mitchell Collection

1970, "It's the real thing," Coca-Cola presented its new image here, one that many collectors don't care to collect, so the demand for 1970 or newer calendars is not great...yet!, M, $20.00. Mitchell Collection

1970, reference edition featuring Santa with a bottle, M, $10.00.

Mitchell Collection

1972, cloth featuring Lillian Nordica, EX, $5.00.

1968, reference edition of Santa on ladder, M $20.00

1970s, tin holder with wave logo at top and tear off day sheets on bottom, EX. $60.00

1971, shadow box with full pad, M. $20.00

1972, "Featuring crafts & hobbies to enjoy with the real thing. Coke," M $15.00

1973, cloth with Lillian Nordica standing by Coca-Cola table, EX, $5.00.

1975, scenes of America showing back packers, with full pad, M, $15.00. Mitchell Collection

1976, "Look up America," "It's the real thing - Coke," with full pad, M, $20.00. Mitchell Collection

1979, Olympic torch, full pad, M, $10.00. Mitchell Collection

1981, "Have a Coke and a smile," full pad with scenes of America at top, EX, $10.00. Mitchell Collection

1974, 1927 reproduction, reverse image, full pad, M. $20.00

1978, air born snow skier, full pad, M $10.00

1980, sports scenes, full pad, M. $10.00

1982, four women around piano, full pad, M $10.00

1983, iced down bottles in front of a bonfire, full pad, M $10.00

Candles TV tray, 1961, 18¾"x13½", EX, $15.00.

Top left: Change, "Drink Coca-Cola Delicious Refreshing," Juanita, 1900, 4" dia, EX, $1,000.00. Top right: Change, World War I Girl, 1916, 4⅜"x6⅛", EX, $325.00. Bottom left: Change, "Drink Coca-Cola, Relieves Fatigue," 1907, EX, $725.00. Bottom right: Change, featuring Betty, 1914, EX, $425.00. Mitchell Collection

Change, "Drink a Bottle of Carbonated Coca-Cola," 1903, 5½" dia, EX, $5,000.00.

Change, featuring Hilda Clark, round, 1903, 6" dia, VG, $2,300.00. Gary Metz

Change, featuring the Coca-Cola Girl by Hamilton King, 1909–10, 4⅜"x6⅛", King, VG, $350.00.

Gary Metz

Canadian, 1957, 14¼"x10½", EX $150.00

Change, Hilda Clark, 1901, 6" dia, VG, $1,250.00.
Gary Metz

Top left: Change, Hamilton King model enjoying a glass, 1913, 4¼"x6", King, EX, $600.00. Top right: Change, oval commemorating the St. Louis World's Fair, 1909, 4¼"x6", EX, $500.00. Bottom left: Change, oval last change tray issued in United States, 1920, EX, $425.00. Bottom right: Change, featuring the Coca-Cola Girl, 1910, King, EX, $550.00. Mitchell Collection

Change, Hilda Clark at table with stationary holding a glass in a glass holder, 1903, 6" dia, EX, $1,700.00.

Change, Hilda Clark seated at table with glass, 1900, 6" dia, EX, $3,000.00.

Change, Hilda Clark, metal, 1903, 4" dia, EX, $2,000.00.

Change, Hilda Clark with flowers, 1901, 6" dia, EX, $2,500.00.

Change receiver, ceramic, with dark lettering and red line outline "The Ideal Brain Tonic, For Headache and Exhaustion," 1899, EX, $5,500.00.

Change receiver, glass, "Drink Coca-Cola 5¢," 1907, 7" dia, EX, $1,100.00.

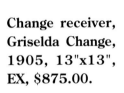

Change receiver, Griselda Change, 1905, 13"x13", EX, $875.00.

Change receiver, Hilda Clark, glass, 1900, 8½" dia, EX, $4,000.00.

Christmas serving tray, there are many variations of this tray, 1973, EX, $10.00.

Change receiver, ceramic, "The Ideal Brain Tonic" with red lettering, 1890s, 10½" dia, EX $4,500.00

"Drink Coca-Cola, Delicious Refreshing," red background with yellow and white lettering, fairly rare, 1940–50s, 12¾" dia, EX $325.00

Serving, Autumn Girl, this model is featured on the 1922 calendar, rectangular, 1920s, 10½"x13¼", EX, $800.00. Mitchell Collection

Serving, Betty, manufactured by Stelad Signs, Passic New Jersey, oval, 1914, 12½"x15¼", EX, $750.00. Beware of reproductions. Mitchell Collection

Serving, boy and dog, boy is holding sandwich and a bottle, 1931, 10½"x13¼", Rockwell, EX, $775.00. Mitchell Collection

Serving, Canadian commemorative with the English version, with Lillian Nordica, 1968, 10½"x13¼", EX, $85.00. Mitchell Collection

Serving, Captain James Cook bicentennial, produced to celebrate the landing at Nootka Sound, B.C, "Coca-Cola" on back, 1978, EX $25.00

Serving, Coca-Cola Girl holding a glass, 1913, 10½"x13¼", King, EX, 900.00. Beware of reproductions. Mitchell Collection

Serving, "Drink Coca-Cola, Delicious and Refreshing," girl on dock, Sailor Girl, 1940, 13¼"x10½", EX, $300.00. Mitchell Collection

Serving, Coca-Cola Girl, oval, 1913, 12¼"x14¼", King, EX, $950.00. Mitchell Collection

Serving, "Coca-Cola" with good litho by Western Coca-Cola Bottling Company of Chicago, Illinois, without the sanction of the Coca-Cola Company, 1908, VG, $4,500.00. Gary Metz

Serving, "Drink Coca-cola, Refreshing Delicious," featuring Hilda Clark, 1900, 9¼" dia, EX, $7,500.00.

Serving, "Drink Coca-Cola Relieves Fatigue," oval, 1907, 10½"x13¼", EX, $2,250.00. Mitchell Collection

Serving, featuring movie star Madge Evans, manufactured by American Art Works, Inc, Coshoctin, Ohio, 1935, 10½"x13¼", EX, $375.00. Mitchell Collection

Serving, featuring a couple receiving curb service, 1927, 13¼"x10½", G, $625.00. Mitchell Collection

Serving, Curb Service for fountain sales, 1928, EX . $675.00

Serving, featuring a pull cart with a picnic basket, 1958, 13¼"x10½", EX, $25.00. Mitchell Collection

Serving, featuring Betty, rectangular, 1914, 10½"x13¼", EX, $775.00. Beware of reproductions.
Mitchell Collection

Serving, featuring bird house full of flowers, French version, 1950s, 10½"x13¼", EX, $110.00. Mitchell Collection

Serving, featuring girl on arm of chair in party dress, Hostess, 1936, 10½"x13¼", EX, $375.00. Mitchell Collection

Serving, featuring girl on beach in chair with a bottle, 1932, 10½"x13¼", EX, $635.00. Mitchell Collection

Serving, featuring Elaine, manufactured by Stelad Signs Passaic Metal Ware Company, Passaic, New Jersey, rectangular, 1916, 8½"x19", EX, $575.00. Beware of reproductions. Mitchell Collection

Serving, "Drive-In," "Drink Coca-Cola" in fishtail logo "Goes good with food" under logo "Drive in for Coke" on rim, a hard to find piece, 1959, VG $125.00

Serving, Edmonton, rectangular, 1978, 10½"x13¼", EX $20.00

Serving, Elaine, 1916, 8½"x19", EX $350.00

Serving, featuring bottle of Coca-Cola with food, Mexican, 1970, 13¼", M $20.00

Serving, featuring girl running on beach with bottles in each hand, 1937, EX, $300.00. Beware of reproductions. Mitchell Collection

Serving, featuring Lillian Nordica on Canadian commemorative, 1968, 10½"x 13¼", EX, $85.00. Mitchell Collection

Serving, featuring ice skaters on log with ice skates and a bottle, 1941, 10½"x13¼", EX, 325.00. Mitchell Collection

Serving, featuring the Coca-Cola Girl, this was the first rectangular tray used by the Coca-Cola Company by American Art Work, Inc., 1909, 10½"x13¼", King, EX, $1100.00. Beware of reproductions. Mitchell Collection

Serving, featuring red headed woman in yellow scarf with a bottle, 1950s, 10½"x13¼", EX, $100.00. Beware of reproductions. Mitchell Collection

Serving, featuring the girl at party, 1921, 10½"x13¼", EX, $475.00. Mitchell Collection

Serving, featuring the famous Maureen O'Sullivan and Johnny Weismuller both holding a bottle, 1934, 13¼"x10½", EX, $800.00. Beware of reproductions. Mitchell Collection

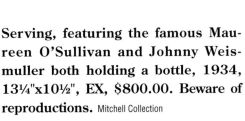

Serving, featuring the movie star, Francis Dee, 1933, 10½"x13¼", EX, $425.00. Mitchell Collection

Serving, featuring the Summer Girl, manufactured by the H. D. Beach Company, Coshoctin, Ohio, 1922, 10½"x13¼", EX, $825.00. Mitchell Collection

Serving, featuring the Smiling Girl holding a glass, this tray can have either a brown or maroon border, add $200.00 for maroon tray, 1924, 10½"x13¼", EX, $675.00. Mitchell Collection

Serving, featuring woman in rain coat with umbrella and a bottle, French version, 1950s, 10½"x13¼", G, $110.00.
Mitchell Collection

Serving, Flapper Girl, 1923, 10½"x13¼", EX, $400.00 Mitchell Collection

Serving, Garden Girl, 1920, 13¼"x16½", EX, $875.00. Mitchell Collection

Serving, French, featuring food and bottles on table, 1957, EX, $100.00. Mitchell Collection

Serving, girl in afternoon with a bottle, produced by American Art Works Inc, Coshoctin, Ohio, 1938, 10½"x13¼", EX, $275.00.

Mitchell Collection

Serving, girl in swimsuit holding bottle, promoting bottle sales, 1929, 10½"x13¼", VG, $600.00.

Serving, girl on a spring board, 1939, 10½"x13¼", EX, $300.00. Mitchell Collection

Serving, Hilda Clark, "Drink Coca-Cola Invigorating, Refreshing, Delicious," 1899, 9¼" dia, EX, $10,500.00.

Serving, Hilda Clark, round, 1903, 9½" dia, NM, $3,200.00. Gary Metz

Serving, Juanita, oval, "Drink Coca-Cola, In Bottles 5¢, at Fountains 5¢," 1906, 10½"x13¼", EX, $2,500.00.

Serving, girl with glass and bottle, Mexican, round, 1965, 13¼" dia, M. $110.00

Serving, "Hambly's Beverage Limited," featuring World War I girl, 60th anniversary, 1977, EX $15.00

Serving, Juanita, bottle version, 1906, 10½"x13½", EX $2,500.00

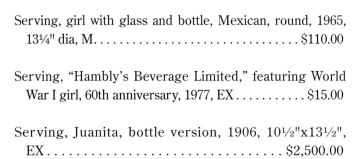

Serving, "Here's a Coke for you," more than three versions of this tray, 1961, 13¼"x10½", EX, $20.00.

Mitchell Collection

Serving, Menu Girl holding a bottle in her hand, 1950s, 10½"x13¼", EX, $75.00. Mitchell Collection

Serving, Menu Girl, French version, 1955 – 60, 10½"x13¼", EX, $100.00.

Serving, Lillian Nordica, "Drink Coca-Cola at Soda Fountains, Delicious Refreshing," oval, 1905, 10½"x13", EX, $4,000.00.

Serving, miscellaneous items, French version, 1950s, 10½"x13¼", G, $110.00. Mitchell Collection

Serving, promoting bottle sales, 1929, 10½"x13¼", F, $450.00.

Mitchell Collection

Serving promoting bottle sales, bobbed hair girl drinking from bottle with a straw, 1928, 10½"x13¼", EX, $650.00. Mitchell Collection

Serving, picnic basket, 1958, 11¼"x10½", EX, $40.00.

Serving, Lillian Nordica, "Drink Carbonated Coca-Cola in Bottles 5¢ Delicious Refreshing," oval, 1905, 10½"x13", EX $4,000.00

Serving, oval, Hilda Clark, 1903, 15"x18½", EX . . $5,100.00

Serving, pansy garden, 1961, 13¼"x10½", EX $25.00

Serving, promoting bottle sales, girl in red swim cap and bathing suit with towel, 1930, EX, $450.00. Mitchell Collection

Serving, promoting fountain sales featuring girl in yellow swim suit, produced by American Art Works Inc. of Coshoctin, Ohio, 1929, 10½"x13¼", EX, $475.00. Mitchell Collection

Serving, promoting fountain sales, girl on phone, "meet me at the soda fountain," 1930, 10½"x13¼", EX, $425.00. Mitchell Collection

Serving, promoting fountain sales with soda person (the term "soda jerk" wasn't used until much later), 1928, 10½"x13¼", EX, $650.00.

Mitchell Collection

Serving, round, "Drink a Bottle of Carbonated Coca-Cola, The Most Refreshing Drink in the World," 1903, 9¾" dia, EX, $6,500.00.

Serving, sports couple, 1926, 10½"x13¼", EX, $725.00. Beware of reproductions. Mitchell Collection

Serving, rectangular, covered bridge with "Coca-Cola" on side, Summer Bridge, 1995, Jim Harrison, EX.... $10.00

Serving, rectangular, "Goodwill Bottling Std," logo in lower right, 1979, EX $15.00

Serving, red-haired girl with wind in hair on solid background, 1950, EX. Beware: Reproductions exist $165.00

Serving, round, featuring University of Indiana basketball, 1976, EX $25.00

Serving, St. Louis Fair, oval, 1909, 13½"x16½", EX, $2,700.00. Mitchell Collection

Serving, two women at car with bottles, because of metal needed in the war effort this was the last tray produced until after World War II, 1942, EX, $325.00.

Mitchell Collection

Serving, Victorian Girl, "Drink Coca-Cola, Refreshing, Delicious," woman drinking from a glass, 1897, 9¼" dia, EX, $14,000.00.

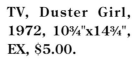

Serving, with Garden Girl, 1920, 10½"x13¼", EX, $750.00. Mitchell Collection

TV, Duster Girl, 1972, 10¾"x14¾", EX, $5.00.

TV, Thanksgiving, 1961, 187¾"x13½", EX, $15.00.

St. Louis Fair, 1909, 10½"x13¼", EX $1,500.00

TV assortment, 1956, 18¾"x13½", EX, $15.00.

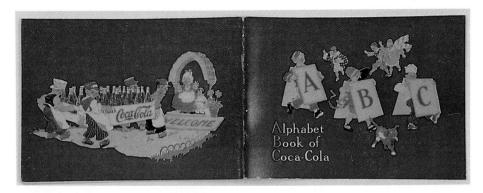

Alphabet Book of Coca-Cola, 1928, EX, $65.00. Mitchell Collection

**Book cover, America is Strong...
because America is Good! with
Dwight Eisenhower on front, 1950s,
EX, $8.00.** Mitchell Collection

Book, *100 Best Posters,* hard cover, 1941, EX $45.00

Book, 1942 advertising price list, 1942, EX, $190.00. Gary Metz

Book, 1943 price list for advertising, 1943, EX, 225.00. Gary Metz

Book, 1944 advertising price list, 1944, $250.00. Gary Metz

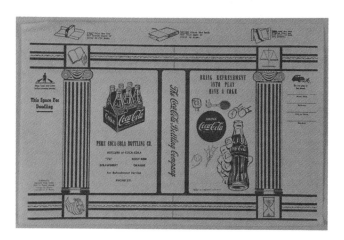

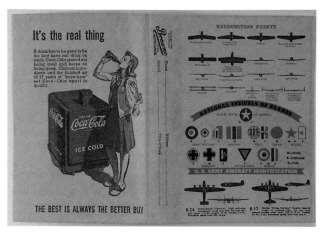

Book cover for school book, 1940–50s, white and red, EX, $8.00. Mitchell Collection

Book cover, national insignia of planes, 1940s, EX, $20.00. Mitchell Collection

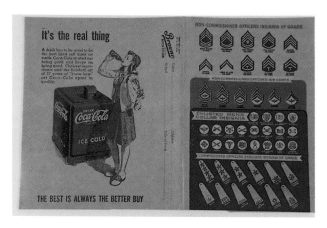

Book cover, Planets and the Stars, 1960s, EX, $20.00. Mitchell Collection

Book cover showing military rank insignias, 1940s, EX, $8.00. Mitchell Collection

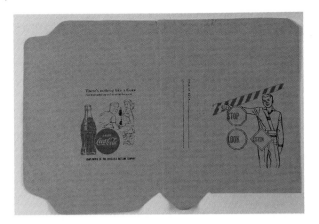

Book cover, "There's nothing like a Coke," school boy, 1940s, EX, $15.00. Mitchell Collection

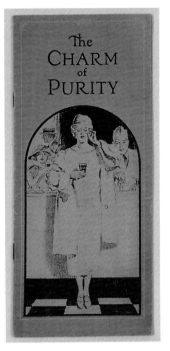

Booklet, The Charm of Purity, 1920s, 35.00.
Mitchell Collection

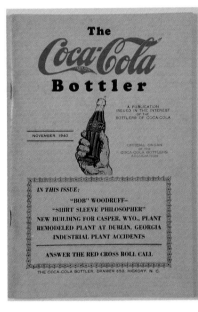

Booklet, The Coca-Cola Bottler, 1940, EX, $30.00. Mitchell Collection

Booklet, Pure and Healthful, 1915, G, $30.00.
Gary Metz

Book, *Illustrated Guide to the Collectibles of Coca-Cola,* Cecil Munsey, 1972, EX. $65.00

Book, *Pause For Living,* bound copy, 1960s, Red, EX. $12.00

Book, six bottle carton with dealer info, 1937, EX. . . $12.00

Book, sugar ration, 1943, EX $25.00

Book, *The 5 Star Book,* 1928, EX $35.00

Book, *The Six Bottle Carton for the Home,* illustrated, 1937, EX $240.00

Book, *The Wonderful World of Coca-Cola,* NM $70.00

Book, *When You Entertain,* by Ida Bailey Allen, 1932, EX $15.00

Booklet, *Easy Hospitality,* 1951, EX $8.00

Booklet, *Facts,* 1923, EX $55.00

Booklet, *Flower Arranging,* 1940, EX $10.00

Booklet, *Homes and Flowers,* 1940, EX $8.00

Booklet, *Know Your War Planes,* 1940s, EX $45.00

Booklet, *Profitable Soda Fountain Operation,* 1953, EX. $65.00

Booklet, *Profitable Soda Fountain Operation,* with Sprite Boy logo on back, 1953, EX $75.00

Booklet, *The Romance of Coca-Cola,* 1916, EX $75.00

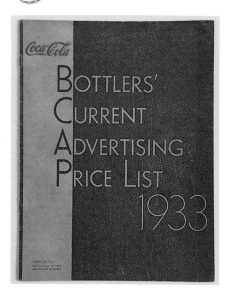

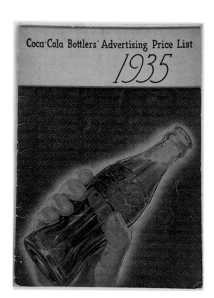

Bottlers' advertising price list, 1933, EX, $190.00. Mitchell Collection

Bottlers' advertising price list, 1935, EX, $200.00. Mitchell Collection

Bottlers' advertising price list, 50th Anniversary, 1936, EX, $250.00. Mitchell Collection

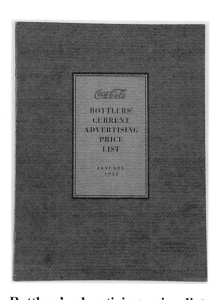

Bottlers' advertising price list, January 1932, 1932, EX, $185.00. Mitchell Collection

Top: Check, Globe Bank and Trust Co, 1907, EX, $15.00. Center: Check, Coca-Cola Bottling Works with bottling plant on left side of check at Sixth and Jackson, Paducah, KY, 1915, EX, $50.00. Bottom: Check, Coca-Cola Bottling Works banner at top and Eagle on top of world globe on left side of check, 1905, EX, $20.00. Mitchell Collection

Booklet with woman in front of sun dial on front and bottle in hand on back cover, with original envelope, 1923, EX. $30.00

Bottlers' magazine, *The Red Barrel,* 1940, EX $15.00

Bulletin book for route men, 1950–60s, VG $25.00

Card hologram, Cal Ripken, McDonalds & Coke, 1991, NM. $8.00

Carton wrap, "Holiday Hospitality," 1940s, M $20.00

Catalog sheet, Roy G. Booker Coca-Cola jewelry from "Gifts In Fine Jewelry," 1940, NM $70.00

Catalog, The All-Star Mechanical Pencil Line, featuring Coca-Cola and other drink lines, 1941, M $45.00

Christmas card with "Seasons Greetings" under silver ornament, 1976, Red, M $5.00

Circus cut out for kids, still uncut in one piece, 1927, EX. $250.00

Circus cut out for kids, uncut in one sheet, 1932, NM. $125.00

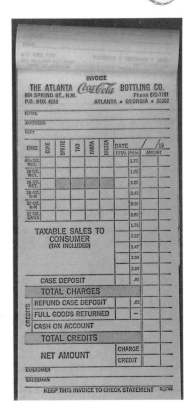

Check, "Globe Bank & Trust Co, Paducah, Ky. signed by Paducah Ky. bottler Luther Carson, 1908, EX, $100.00. Mitchell Collection

Coupon for 5¢, EX, $15.00. Mitchell Collection

Driver's route book, EX, $5.00.

Coupon, Free Coke with Sprite Boy, 1950s, VG, $12.00. Mitchell Collection

Comic book, "Refreshment Through The Ages," 1951, EX $25.00

Comic trade card featuring woman in bathtub and serving bottles from a serving tray, 1905. Beware: Reproductions exist $800.00

Convention packet, 14th Annual Coca-Cola Convention at Philadelphia, 1988, MIB $30.00

Coupon, 1900, EX $400.00

Coupon, featured 12 pack, 1950s, EX $8.00

Coupon, "Free 6 Bottles of Coca-Cola," pictures six pack with wire handle, 1950s, EX $5.00

Coupon, free bottle of Coke, 1920s, EX. $15.00

Coupon, Free Coke at soda fountain, 1908, EX $225.00

Coupon, Hilda Clark, 1901, EX. $500.00

Coupon, Lillian Nordica, 1905, 6½"x9¾", EX $250.00

Coupon, "Refresh yourself," Free at Roberts & Echols, Glendale Calif, 1920s, 5"x2", EX $35.00

Coupon, "Take home a carton," 1930s, EX. $30.00

Coupon, "This card entitles an adult to one glass of Coca-Cola Free," 1890s, EX $250.00

Coupon, "This Card Entitles You To One Glass of Coca-Cola," 1903, EX. $400.00

Coupon, "Wholesome Refreshment" with red headed boy drinking from a bottle with a straw, 1920s, EX $20.00

Coupons, "Refresh Yourself" with bottle in hand, 1920s, EX. $20.00

Coupons, soda person "Refresh Yourself," 1927, 2¼"x4", EX $85.00

Display sheet for cartons, "Match The Brides...for Fun and Prizes," for 35 cap display, 1967, EX. $20.00

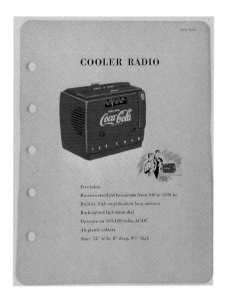

Fact sheet from bottlers book for cooler radio, 1950s, VG, $75.00. Mitchell Collection

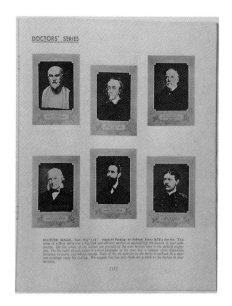

Famous Doctors Series, set of six heavy folders, complete, of individual figure approximately $30.00 each, 1932, EX, $190.00. Mitchell Collection

Halloween promotional package for dealers, 1954, EX, $20.00. Mitchell Collection

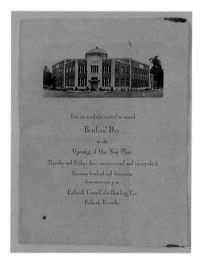

Invitation to attend the opening of the Paducah, KY, Coca-Cola plant, with picture of the bottling plant at top of sheet, 1939, G, $25.00. Mitchell Collection

Holder for gas ration book, "Drink Coca-Cola in Bottles," G, $20.00. Mitchell Collection

Magazine cover, front and back, The Housewife, June 1910, framed, The A. D. Poster Co, Publisher, New York, 1910, G, $165.00. Mitchell Collection

Health record, My Daily Reminder, Compliments of Sanford Coca-Cola Bottling Co, Sanford, N.C. Phone 20, 1930s, EX. $12.00

Information kit, New York World's Fair, "The Coca-Cola Company Pavilion," 1964, NM $50.00

Kit, merchandising for cooler, 1930, M. $85.00

Letter, Asa G. Chandler, framed and matted, 1889, EX. $175.00

Magazine, *The Coca-Cola™ Bottler,* 1940s, EX. $20.00

Magazine, vest pocket, complete set of 52, 1928, NM $500.00

Magazine, *Pause for Living,* a single copy, 1960, EX . . $3.00

Menu, for soda fountain, framed and matted, 1902, 4⅛"x6⅛", EX $600.00

Menu, Hilda Clark, rare, 1901, 11¾"x4", EX $1,200.00

Menu sheet from the 1930s – 1950s in a menu holder from the 1960s, 1930s–1960s, VG, $25.00. Mitchell Collection

Newspaper, Paducah Sun-Democrat, June 18, 1939, advertising the opening of a new bottling plant, F, $50.00.

Mitchell Collection

Top: Money roll, quarters, M, $6.00. Bottom: Money roll, halves, $6.00. Mitchell Collection

Menu, Hilda Clark, soda menu, framed and matted, hard to find, 1903, 4⅛"x6⅛", EX $650.00

Menu, Lillian Nordica, framed and matted, 1904, 4⅛"x6½", EX $650.00

Napkin with Sprite Boy, 1950s, M $10.00

Note pad, celluloid, 1902, 2½"x5", EX. $600.00

Note pad, green alligator cover, "Compliments the Coca-Cola Co" stamped on front in gold, 1906, EX $225.00

Note pad, Hilda Clark, framed and matted, 1903, 2½"x5", EX $600.00

Note pad holder, calf skin, 1946, EX $25.00

Note pad, leather covered, 1905, 2¾"x4½", EX $225.00

Price list with great colors and period graphics in book form, 1941, EX, $325.00. Gary Metz

Note pad with boy and dog, 1931, 10"x7", Rockwell, EX $35.00

Notebook, "Coca-Cola Advertised Schedule," 1980, EX . $10.00

Olympiad Records wheel, 1932, EX. $100.00

Opera program presented by Columbus Coca-Cola Bottling Co, 1906, EX $100.00

Placemats, "Around The World," set of four, 1950s, EX . $12.00

Pocket secretary, hard bound, 1920s, EX $30.00

Score pads, "Spotter," "Drink Coca-Cola Delicious
and Refreshing," and military nurse in uniform,
1940, EX, $10.00 each. Mitchell Collection

School book cover with Sprite Boy, 1940–50s,
EX, $5.00. Mitchell Collection

Punch card for a "Bottle Coke" Special,
with punches of 1, 2, 3, 4, and 5 cents
manufactured by W. H. Hardy Co, Eau
Claire, Wisc, 1900, VG, $5.00. Mitchell Collection

Route coupon from
Paducah, Ky, EX,
$15.00. Mitchell Collection

Return ticket showing price
of returned bottle deposit,
G, $10.00. Mitchell Collection

Rand McNally Auto Road Map of Illinois with a Coca-
Cola advertisement on the back cover, 1920s,
$35.00. Mitchell Collection

Report card holder with 1923 bottle, 1930s, EX $85.00

School kit, Man & His Environment, 1970s, EX $22.00

Score pad, American Women's Volunteer Service, 1940s,
    EX $15.00

Sheet music, cover and song sheet, *I'd Like to Buy the
    World A Coke™,* 1971, 8½"x11½", EX $25.00

Sheet music, *It's the Real Thing,* 1969, EX $10.00

Sheet music, *Rum & Coca-Cola,* Jeri Sullivan, EX . . . $20.00

Souvenirs, Confederate Bank note, 1931, EX $75.00

Toonerville cut out still uncut and in one piece, 1930,
    M $45.00

Sheet music for the Coca-Cola Girl, words and music by Howard E. Way, published by The Coca-Cola Company, Atlanta, Ga, U.S.A, framed, 1927, VG, $325.00. Mitchell Collection

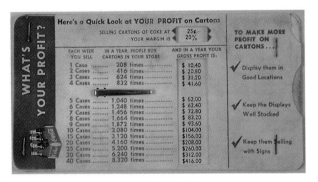

Slide chart for figuring profits on sales of Coca-Cola, G, $10.00. Mitchell Collection

Slide information booklet, Kit Carson, 1950s, VG, $35.00. Mitchell Collection

Writing tablet featuring Sprite Boy and safety ABC's, 1950s, EX $6.00

Writing tablet, flags, 1960s, EX $5.00

Writing tablet, landmarks of the U.S.A, 1960s, EX.... $6.00

Writing tablet, Pure As Sunlight, 1930s, EX $20.00

Writing tablet, wildlife of the United States, 1970s, EX . $5.00

Sheet music of My Old Kentucky Home featuring Juanita on cover with a glass, 1906, EX, $850.00.

Sheet music, Rock me to Sleep Mother, with Juanita on cover drinking from a glass, 1906, EX, $875.00.

Wild flower study cards for schools, complete set consists of 20 cards and envelopes, 1920–30, VG, $60.00 set.

Writing tablet, with Silhouette Girl, 1940s, EX...... $10.00

Fans

Bamboo with front and back graphics, "Keep Cool, Drink Coca-Cola," Oriental lady drinking a glass of Coca-Cola on opposite side, 1900, VG, $150.00. Mitchell Collection

Cardboard fold out from the Coca-Cola Bottling Co, Bethlehem, Pennsylvania, 1950s, EX, $45.00. Mitchell Collection

Cardboard fold out with Sprite Boy from the Coca-Cola bottler at Memphis, Tenn, 1951, F, $50.00. Mitchell Collection

Cardboard foldout from the Atlanta Coca-Cola Bottling Company, EX, $50.00. Mitchell Collection

Cardboard on wooden handle, "Enjoy Coca-Cola," 1960s, EX, $15.00. Mitchell Collection

Cardboard and wood with picture of a mother and child, "Drive with care, protect our loved ones" $110.00

Cardboard on wooden handle, with Sprite Boy, "Have A Coke," 1950s, EX, $55.00. Mitchell Collection

Cardboard with rolled paper handle, with poem on cover, 1930s, EX, $135.00. Mitchell Collection

Cardboard with rolled paper handle, "Drink Coca-Cola the Pause that Refreshes," 1930, $155.00. Mitchell Collection

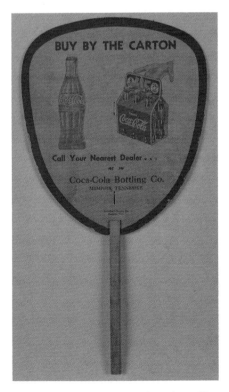

Cardboard with wooden handle, "Buy by the carton, 6 for 25¢," Memphis, Tenn, 1930s, EX, $60.00. Mitchell Collection

Cardboard with wooden handle, "Drink Coca-Cola" with bottle in spot light, 1930s, EX, $75.00. Mitchell Collection

Cardboard with wooden handle from the Coca-Cola Bottling Works of Greenwood Mississippi, "Enjoy Coca-Cola," 1960s, EX, $15.00. Mitchell Collection

Cardboard with wooden handle, Sprite Boy, "A way to win a welcome whenever you go," Starr Bros. Coca-Cola Bottling Company, Mt. Vernon, Illinois, 1950s, $110.00. Mitchell Collection

"Drink Coca-Cola" featuring a spotlighted bottle with wooden handle, 1930s, EX, $65.00. Mitchell Collection

Cardboard with wooden handle, Sprite Boy, "Bottles, Bottles Who's got the Empty Bottles?," Paducah Coca-Cola Bottling Company, Inc, 1950s, EX, $100.00. Mitchell Collection

Paper with wooden handle, spotlight on bottle in center, 1950s, EX, $60.00. Mitchell Collection

Paper on wooden handle manufactured by Franklin-Cora Co Richmond, Va, "Chew Coca-Cola Gum," red lettering on white background, 1912–16, VG, $2,000.00.

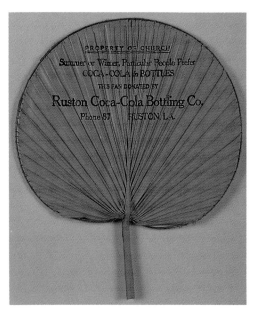

Property of Church, donated by Ruston Coca-Cola Bottling Co, Ph 87, Ruston, La, 1920s, EX, $75.00. Mitchell Collection

"Quality carries on, Drink Coca-Cola" with bottle in hand, 1950, EX, $50.00. Mitchell Collection

Rolled paper handle, "Drink Coca-Cola The Pause That Refreshes," Coca-Cola Bottling Co. Martin, Tenn, Phone 411, EX, $100.00. Mitchell Collection

Wicker, compliments of Waycross Coca-Cola Bottling Co, 1950s, EX, $55.00. Mitchell Collection

Blotters

50th Anniversary, 1936, EX $65.00

"A pure drink of natural flavors," 1929, EX $150.00

"Be Prepared," 1950, EX $20.00

Bottle in hand over the earth, 1958, EX $10.00

Bottle, large, "Over 60 million a Day," 1960, EX $8.00

Bottle, paper label, "The Most Refreshing Drink in the World," 1904, EX $350.00

Boy Scouts, "Wholesome Refreshment," 1942, EX ... $8.00

Canadian, 1940, NM $30.00

"Carry A Smile Back To Work Feeling Fit," 1935, M . $95.00

Coca-Cola being enjoyed by a policeman, 1938, EX. . $25.00

"Coke Knows No Season," snow scene, great graphics, 1947, EX $15.00

"Cold Refreshment," 1937, EX $30.00

"The Pause That Refreshes," 1930, EX, $40.00. Gary Metz

"Completely Refreshing," with disk upper left, 1942, EX $30.00

Couples at a party, Canadian, 1955, EX $20.00

"Delicious and Refreshing," fountain service, 1915, EX $185.00

"Delicious, Refreshing, Invigorating," 1909, Red & White, EX $110.00

"Delicious, Refreshing," Sprite Boy and a bottle, 1951, EX $8.00

Left, from top: "So Refreshing, Keep on Ice," couple at ice box, 1927, M, $60.00; "Refresh Yourself," white haired gentleman in hat looking at bottle, 1928, $75.00; "Be Prepared, be Refreshed," Boy Scout at cooler with a bottle in each hand, 1940s, M, $15.00. Right, from top: "And one for you," girl on blanket holding bottle, 1934, $85.00; Boy with fishing pole and dog drinking from a bottle, 1930s, $85.00; "Good with food. Try It," plate of food with two bottles, 1930s, M, $50.00. Mitchell Collection

"Drink Coca-Cola," Atlanta, 1904, EX $400.00

"Drink Coca-Cola," Chicago, 1904, EX $110.00

"Drink...Delicious & Refreshing All Soda Fountain 5 cents," 1915, EX $175.00

Fountain sales, 1913, EX $40.00

"Friendliest drink on earth," a bottle in hand, 1956, 4"x8", EX $10.00

Full set of six , different poses, 1970s, EX $250.00

Girl in boat, 1942, EX $20.00

Girl laying on her stomach, 1942, EX $20.00

"I Think It's Swell," 1944, 3½"x7½", EX $10.00

" I Think It's Swell," girl, 1942, EX $8.00

Policeman with bottle, 1938, EX $65.00

"Pure and Healthful," with a paper label on each side to promote bottle sales, 1913, EX $40.00

"Pure and Healthful," with bottles on both sides, 1916, G $35.00

"Refresh Yourself," 1926, EX $35.00

"Refreshing & Delicious" disc, 1940, EX $30.00

"Restores Energy," 1906, red and white, EX $130.00

Sprite Boy, 1947, EX $90.00

Sprite Boy with a bottle in the snow, 1953, EX $8.00

"The Drink Everyone Knows," 1939, EX $35.00

"The Greatest Pause On Earth," 1940, EX $75.00

"The most refreshing drink in the world," 1905, EX. $200.00

"The Pause That Refreshes," 1929, EX $85.00

"The Pause That Refreshes," 1930, EX $50.00

"The Pause That Refreshes," 1931, EX $225.00

Three girls with bottles, disc at right, 1944, NM $30.00

International truck, VG, $15.00. Mitchell Collection

Coca-Cola Bottling Co, No 1 at Paducah, KY, with picture of bottling plant at Sixth and Jackson St, 1920s, $35.00. Mitchell Collection

Auto delivery truck with an even loaded bed and five men on board, 1913, EX $135.00

Bobby Allison & Coke, 1970s, NM $8.00

Bottling plant showing interior, 1905, EX $125.00

Coca-Cola™ girl, 1910, Hamilton King, EX $700.00

Duster girl, 1911, 3½"x5½", EX $700.00

Exterior of a bottling plant showing the truck fleet in front of building, 1906, EX $150.00

Folding, "Have You a Hobby?," showing a youngster on a rocking horse, 1910, EX $175.00

Folding, "Will You Have It - When They Call?," 1913, EX $135.00

Free six bottles with wire handled carton commemorating 65th Anniversary, 1950s, EX $10.00

Horse-drawn delivery wagon, 1900, EX $125.00

Horse-drawn delivery wagon with a Coca-Cola umbrella, 1913, EX $130.00

Interior of store, 1904, EX $100.00

International truck, 1940s, EX $8.00

Motorized delivery wagon with three men standing beside it, 1915, EX $125.00

Photo truck loaded with case of Coca-Cola in snow, framed, 1910, 8"x10", black and white, EX $100.00

Post card featuring picture of DuQuoin, Illinois, bottling plant, NM $30.00

Race car of Bobby Allison, 1973, EX $8.00

Store showing bar with ceramic dispensers and pool table, 1904, EX $100.00

The Fulton Coca-Cola Bottling Co, 1909, EX $150.00

Trifold, showing profit for selling Coca-Cola, featuring a teacher at blackboard, 1910s, EX $450.00

Trifold, showing profits sitting on top of globe, 1913, EX $150.00

Weldmech truck, 1930, EX $8.00

Ads

Magazine, "Even the bubbles taste better," 1956, VG, $3.00.

American, man and woman toasting each other with flare glasses inside a large flare glass, NM $8.00

"Baseball and Coke grew up together," young boy in uniform with a bottle, framed, 1951, 12"x15", NM. $8.00

Delineator featuring a city scene, 1921, EX. $8.00

"Drink" with a glass on ledge in foreground, 1917, EX $12.00

"Face the Day Refreshed" with woman at table and "Drink..." button in upper left framed, 1939, 12"x15", EX $12.00

"Get together with refreshment," couple at soda fountain, "Drink..." button upper right, framed and matted, 1941, 12"x15", NM $10.00

Girl with flare glass, 1910s, EX. $8.00

Girl with muffler, 1923, NM $20.00

"Has Character," featuring soda person, 1913, VG . . . $8.00

Magazine, Sprite Boy looking at Santa in front of opened refrigerator, 1948, EX, $25.00.

Human Life, color, arrow encircling lady, 1910, NM . $85.00

Human Life, color, "Come In" with arrow encircling soda fountain, 1909, NM. $55.00

Ladies' Home Journal, "Enjoy Thirst," girl with straw and bottle, 1923, EX $8.00

Ladies' Home Journal, girl with background showing golfers, 1922, EX $15.00

Ladies' Home Journal, snow scene and skiers with hand in flare glass, 1922, EX. $8.00

Ladies' Home Journal, "Thirst Knows No Season" with calendar girl, December, 1922, EX $20.00

"Let's Get a Coca-Cola," featuring couple under a fountain service sign, framed, 1939, 12"x15", EX $12.00

Magazine, buggy, 1906, EX $35.00

Magazine, featuring Lillian Nordica and a Coke, matted and framed, 1904, NM. $110.00

National Geographic, cover, back, "You Taste It's Quality," 1951, F, $3.00.

Magazine, Sprite Boy at soda fountain wearing soda fountain hat, 1949, G, $25.00.

Magazine, golfing couple, 1906, EX. $110.00

Magazine, "Scorching Hot Day," arrow above test, 1909, EX. $35.00

Massengale, lady and maid, 1906, EX $110.00

"Pause and refresh," three girls in car seat with window tray on window, "Drink..." button upper right corner, 1938, 12"x15", NM $15.00

"Pause...and shop refreshed," couple of ladies at table with glasses, 1940, 12"x15", NM. $8.00

People waiting behind counter, framed and matted, 1905, 14"x10", EX. $120.00

"Refreshment through the years," "Drink..." button lower right, 1951, 12"x15", EX. $8.00

Saturday Evening Post featuring black background and water skier, EX $8.00

Seated girl, 1915, 14"x19", EX $140.00

The Housekeeper cover, front and back, August 1909, framed, 1909, VG, $150.00. Mitchell Collection

"Through 65 Years," left side pictures 1886 fountain service, right side 1951 fountain service, framed, 1951, 12"x15", NM $10.00

Woman's World, 1920, EX $35.00

Bottles

25th Anniversary, 1974, EX, $100.00.

Mitchell Collection

Biedenharm Candy Co, Vicksburg, Miss, embossed lettering, block print on crown top bottle, 1900s, aqua, EX, $200.00.

Biedenharm Candy Co, Vicksburg, Miss, with script "Coca-Cola" on base edge, all embossed, 1905, aqua, EX, $130.00.

Biedenharm Candy Company, Vicksburg, Miss, embossed block print, Hutchinson Bottle, 1894–02, aqua, EX, $250.00.

Block print embossed on base with fluted sides, 7 oz, clear, EX, $40.00.

Block print embossed on shoulder, bottle is unusual due to size and color, 32 oz, green, EX, $55.00.

75th Anniversary, Paducah Coca-Cola Bottling Company, Inc, 1978, 10 oz, clear, EX $15.00

75th Anniversary, Thomas Bottling Company, 1974, amber, EX $75.00

America's Cup, 1987, NM. $45.00

Atlanta Christian College, 1987, 10 oz, NM $8.00

Atlanta Falcons, NM $8.00

Atlanta Olympics, 1996, NM. $5.00

Biedenharm Candy Company with applied paper label and "Coca-Cola" in script on bottle shoulder, 1905, aqua, EX $175.00

Block print "Coca-Cola" in center of bottle body, fluted above and below name, EX $20.00

Block print embossed on side in circle from Sedalia, MO, 6½", aqua, EX, $35.00.

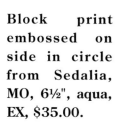

Block print on base, embossed, 6½ oz, aqua, EX, $25.00.

Block print on shoulder, C.C.B. Co. from Raton, NM, embossed, 6 oz, aqua, EX, $25.00.

Canadian with white lettering on clear glass with screw on top, 40oz, clear, EX, $30.00.

Carbonation tester used before the introduction of pre-mix, extremely hard to locate since normally only the bottlers had these items, EX, $500.00.

Ceramic syrup jug with paper label, tall, two-color stoneware, hardest to find, 1900s, 10" tall, VG, $2,600.00. Gary Metz

Brickyard 400 Nascar Inaugural at Indianapolis, NM . $50.00

Cal Ripken, "The Record Breaking Year," NM $3.00

Can, alternating red and white diamonds, red "Coca-Cola" next to white "Coke" on center diamond, 1960s, VG. $50.00

Can, experimental fashioned to feel like bottle, red and white Coca-Cola logo, not put into production, 1970s, 12 oz, NM. $375.00

Can, fashioned to feel like a bottle, white with the dynamic wave logo, experimental only, not put into production, 1970s, 12 oz, NM $250.00

Carolina Panthers #1, NM $3.00

Convention, 1981, EX, $40.00. Although not strictly a Coca-Cola item, these bottles are collected by most Coke collectors and I had several requests to include them here. Mitchell Collection

Convention, 1976, EX, $45.00. Mitchell Collection

Convention, 50th Anniversary National Soft Drink Association, 1969, EX, 100.00. Mitchell Collection

Convention, Anaheim, CA, 1985, EX, $40.00. Mitchell Collection

Convention, Anaheim, CA, 1977, EX, $75.00. Mitchell Collection

Convention, Atlanta, GA, 1994, EX, $25.00. Mitchell Collection

Casey's General Store 25th Anniversary 1968 – 1993, NM $135.00

Clear syrup with metal lid, "Drink Coca-Cola" with outline etched in bottle, 1920s, clear, VG $450.00

Clemson, 1981, NM. $5.00

Commemorative Hutchinson style, "Coca-Cola 1894 – 1979," 1979, 7¼" h, M $35.00

Commemorative reproduction of 1927 bottle used on luxury liners, green glass with green and red label, foil covered neck and top, 1994, M. $65.00

Convention, Atlanta, GA, 1988, EX, $30.00. Mitchell Collection

Convention, Atlanta, GA, 1982, EX, $40.00. Mitchell Collection

Convention, Atlanta, GA, 1978, EX, $45.00. Mitchell Collection

Convention, Atlantic City, NJ, 1966, EX, $50.00. Mitchell Collection

Convention, Atlantic City, NJ, 1962, EX, $65.00. Mitchell Collection

Convention, Atlantic City, NJ, 1952, EX, $125.00. Mitchell Collection

Convention, Atlantic City, NJ, 1958, EX, $95.00. Mitchell Collection

Convention, Chicago, IL, 1992, EX, $25.00. Mitchell Collection

Convention, Chicago, IL, 1990, EX, $25.00. Mitchell Collection

Convention, Chicago, IL, 1987, EX, $30.00. Mitchell Collection

Convention, Chicago, IL, 1984, EX, $40.00. Mitchell Collection

Convention, Chicago, IL, 1980, EX, $40.00. Mitchell Collection

Convention, Chicago, IL, 1972, EX, $45.00. Mitchell Collection

Convention, Chicago, IL, 1964, EX, $55.00. Mitchell Collection

Convention, Chicago, IL, 1953, EX, $100.00. Mitchell Collection

Convention, Cleveland, OH, 1956, EX, $95.00. Mitchell Collection

Convention, Dallas, TX, 1986, EX, 35.00. Mitchell Collection

Convention, Dallas, TX, 1979, EX, 45.00. Mitchell Collection

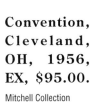

Convention, Dallas, TX, 1975, EX, $5.00. Mitchell Collection

Convention, Dallas, TX, 1963, EX, $60.00. Mitchell Collection

Convention, Detroit, MI, 1968, EX, $50.00. Mitchell Collection

Convention, Detroit, MI, 1960, EX, $80.00. Mitchell Collection

Convention, Houston, TX, 1983, EX, $40.00. Mitchell Collection

Convention, Houston, TX, 1971, EX, $45.00. Mitchell Collection

Convention, Houston, TX, 1967, EX, $50.00. Mitchell Collection

Convention, Las Vegas, NV, 1989, EX, $30.00. Mitchell Collection

Convention, Miami, FL, 1973, EX, $45.00. Mitchell Collection

Convention, Miami, FL, 1965, EX, $50.00. Mitchell Collection

Convention, Miami, FL, 1955, EX, $95.00. Mitchell Collection

Convention, Philadelphia, PA, 1970, EX, $50.00. Mitchell Collection

Convention, Philadelphia, PA, 1954, EX, $95.00. Mitchell Collection

Convention, San Francisco, CA, 1961, EX, $70.00. Mitchell Collection

Convention, San Francisco, CA, 1950, EX, $700.00. Mitchell Collection

Convention, St. Louis, MO, 1959, EX, $85.00. Mitchell Collection

Convention, Washington, D.C., 1957, $90.00. Mitchell Collection

Convention, Washington, D.C., 1951, EX, $125.00. Mitchell Collection

From left: Double diamond with script "Coca-Cola" inside diamond from Toledo, Ohio, 1900–10s, 6 oz., amber, EX, $110.00; Script "Coca-Cola" on bottom edge of front side, on reverse "This bottle our private property & protected by registration under senate bill No. 130 approved June 7th, 1911," Dayton, Ohio, 1900 – 10, 6 oz., amber, EX, $175.00; Script "Coca-Cola" inside arrow circle, Louisville, Ky., 1910s, 6 oz., amber, EX, $75.00; Script "Coca-Cola" on shoulder of bottle with vertical arrow, Cincinnati, Ohio, registered on bottom in block print, 1910s, 6 oz., amber, EX, $100.00.

Embossed script "Coca-Cola" at edge of base with unusual shoulder, clear, EX, $65.00.

Cub Foods, NM $25.00

Detroit Red Wings, NM $3.00

Display bottle with cap and patent date, 1923, 20" tall, EX $450.00

Embossed 24 set, yellow wooden case with red lettering, 1920s, 24 bottle case, yellow, EX $150.00

Florida Forest Festival, 1995, NM $45.00

Florida Marlins, 1994, NM $3.00

Gator Bowl, NM. $4.00

Glass jug with diamond paper label, 1910, one gal, Clear, EX $250.00

Glass jug with hoops at neck and embossed lettering, "Coca-Cola" in script, fairly rare, 1900s, one gal, clear, EX $1,200.00

Gold, 100th Anniversary, 1986, EX, $45.00. Mitchell Collection

Gold, 50th Anniversary 1899 – 1949, Everett Pidgeon in bottle cradle, 1949, EX, $200.00.
Mitchell Collection

Glass jug with paper label, 1960s, one gal, clear, EX . $15.00

Miniature plastic case with all bottles, 1960s, EX, $75.00.

Miniature perfume bottle with glass stopper, 1930s, clear, EX, $65.00. Beware: Reproductions exist.

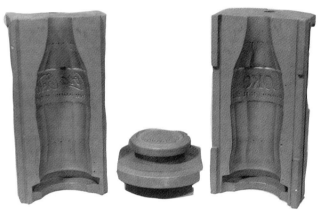

Mold made of solid iron, for 10 oz. no return bottle, very heavy, EX, $375.00. Gary Metz

Glass jug with round paper label, 1910s, one gal, clear, EX $300.00

Glass syrup jug with applied label, 1950, one gal, clear, VG. $20.00

Gold bottle of Bellingrath Gardens & Homes, Mobile, Ala, limited edition, NM $28.00

Gold dipped, "Bottled from the one millionth gallon December 22, 1959 by the Coca-Cola Bottling Co, Memphis Tennessee," 1959, NM $25.00

Guam Liberation Day $10.00

Happy Holidays, 1994, NM. $3.00

Hawaii Mickey Mouse Teentown limited edition, 1994, NM. $12.00

Head Yai, Thailand, new bottling plant, rare, 1993, 10 oz, NM. $85.00

Hutchinson style, "Birmingham Coca-Cola Bottling Co," "DOC 13" on back, 1894, 7" h, NM $1,000.00

Jeff Gordon Winston Cup Champion, 1995, NM $3.00

Lamp with embossed "Coca-Cola" base, 1970s, 20", EX. $6,000.00

Leaded glass display, 1920s, 36" tall, EX $9,500.00

Los Angeles Olympics set in boxes with tags, 1984. $100.00

Mardi Gras, 1996, NM $3.00

Mexico, Christmas with Santa and girl, NM $6.00

Miniature six pack of gold-plated metal bottles, 1970, EX $10.00

Monsanto experimental with screw on lid in various colors, 1960, EX $40.00

North Dakota, embossed Coke with bottle in diamond, 10 oz, NM. $10.00

Orlando World Cup, NM. $3.00

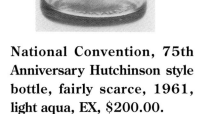

Left: Oklahoma Anniversary, regular capped, gold dipped with white lettering, dated 1903 – 1967 on reverse, only 1,000 made make this a fairly scarce item, 1967, 6½ oz., gold, EX, $100.00. Right: Regular capped gold dipped, embossed lettering, these were made for individual bottlers for special occasions, 6 oz., gold, EX, $25.00.

National Convention, 75th Anniversary Hutchinson style bottle, fairly scarce, 1961, light aqua, EX, $200.00.

"Property of Coca-Cola Bottling Co, La Grange, Texas," in block print on body with embossed ribbon on shoulder, 6 oz, aqua, EX, $30.00. Mitchell Collection

Pete Rose, NM $75.00

Pharmor, NM $275.00

Root Commemorative in box with gold clasp, 1965, aqua, EX $450.00

Root Commemorative in box with silver clasp, 1971, aqua, EX $350.00

San Diego Padres, 1993, NM $3.00

San Francisco 49ers, NM $3.00

Santa Claus Christmas bottle carrier sleeve, Santa Claus & Christmas Greetings, 1930s, M $1,900.00

Premix, 1920s, Green, EX, $55.00.

Mitchell Collection

Original paper label with script "Coca-Cola Beverage," reproduction labels are available, 1900–10, aqua, F, $100.00.

From left: Script "Coca-Cola" at bottom from any location, 1910s, 6 oz, amber, EX, $45.00; Script "Coca-Cola" on base edge, "Bottling WKS 2nd Registered" in block print at bottom of base, 1910s, 6½ oz, amber, EX, $100.00; Script "Coca-Cola" midway from any location, 1910s, 6 oz, amber, EX, $50.00; Script "Coca-Cola" on shoulder from any location, 1910s, 6 oz, Amber, EX, $55.00.

"Root" commemorative bottle is a reissue of the original bottle design of 1915. The original bottle bottoms were plain, the reissue is so marked only 5,000 of the reissues were made, 1965, $415.00. Mitchell Collection

Script "Coca-Cola" in shoulder from Verner Springs Water Co, Greenville, SC, 9", aqua, EX, $55.00.

Script "Coca-Cola" on shoulder and Biedenharm in script on base, all lettering is embossed, 1900s, aqua, $135.00.

Script "Coca-Cola" embossed on body with embossed art around name, 1910–20s, aqua, $75.00.

Mitchell Collection

Seltzer, clear, Royal Palm, Coca-Cola Bottling Co, Terre Haute, Indiana, 1930–40s, EX, $125.00. Mitchell Collection

Seltzer, Coca-Cola Bottling Co, Morgantown, WV, clear with red lettering, VG, $150.00. Gary Metz

Seltzer, clear, from Coca-Cola Bottling Co, Cairo, Illinois, with applied color labeling featuring Ritz boy with tray, EX, $225.00. Mitchell Collection

Seltzer, from Bradford Pennsylvania Bottling Company, blue, VG $110.00

Seltzer, green fluted for Rock Springs Coca-Cola Bottling Company, Rock Springs Wyoming, green, VG . . . $240.00

Seltzer, top marked "Coca-Cola B. Co. R.t. Ill," 1930s, amber, NM $200.00

Seltzer, with etched lettering, dark blue, EX $175.00

Six miniature perfume bottles in miniature 50s style case, 1950s, EX. $160.00

Small tray bottle for toy cooler, 1951, 3½" tall, EX . . . $15.00

St. Louis Rams, NM. $3.00

Standard top, with "Coca-Cola" in block print from Mt. Vernon, IL, embossed at base, 6 oz, aqua, EX $10.00

Straight-sided amber marked "Made at Williamstown, New Jersey" and "Made by Williamstown Glass Company," made by a mold, very rare, 1905–10, 3¼" tall, EX. $3,200.00

Seltzer, Fargo, North Dakota, EX, $200.00. Mitchell Collection

Seltzer, green fluted with good etching, VG, $200.00. Gary Metz

Styrofoam display, 1961, 42" tall, VG. $210.00

Super Bowl 28, NM $3.00

Syrup, with fired on foil label, red lettering on white label, 1920s, NM. $775.00

Syrup, with applied label and original cap, $1,000.00. Gary Metz

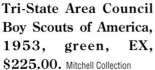

Tri-State Area Council Boy Scouts of America, 1953, green, EX, $225.00. Mitchell Collection

The Coca-Cola Bottling Company, six-sided body, 1920–30, aqua, EX, $50.00. Mitchell Collection

Syrup, with original metal cap, 1920s, EX, $550.00.

Mitchell Collection

White lettering on clear glass with tight fitting plastic top, used as a display piece, 1960s, 20" tall, clear, EX, $65.00.

"Tour the World with Caps from Coke," bottle cap collection three fold out folder, 1950s, VG, $85.00. Mitchell Collection

Syrup can with paper label, 1930s, one gal, red, EX . $200.00

Syrup can with paper label featuring Coca-Cola glass, 1940, EX $325.00

Syrup can with paper label red on white, 1950s, one gal, VG $175.00

Syrup, with "Drink Coca-Cola" inside etched ribbon with bow at bottom, metal lid, 1910, clear, EX. $800.00

Syrup, with foil label red script lettering on white background with gold outline, with original metal lid, 1920, blue, EX. $850.00

Syrup, with paper label "Coca-Cola" in block lettering, metal lid, 1900, clear, EX $700.00

"Tell City, IND," green, 28oz, 1937, 12"h, NM $35.00

Test for 16 oz, "QC" on bottom for quality control, original sticker, scarce due to unusual size, 1940–60s, 16 oz, NM $85.00

Wal-Mart Christmas, 1994, NM $3.00

Wooden keg with paper label, 1920–30, 10 gal, VG . $225.00

Wooden keg with paper label on end, 1920–30s, 5 gal, VG $200.00

York Rite Masonary, NM $20.00

50th Anniversary, gold-dipped with plastic stand, 1950s, EX, $250.00. Gary Metz

Bell, with "Enjoy," set of four different sizes, EX, $12.00.

Arrow flare, small, acid etched with syrup line at bottom, "Drink Coca-Cola 5¢," 1912–13, $675.00. Gary Metz

Flare with syrup line, 1900s, EX, $435.00; Flare, "Bottle Coca-Cola," 1916, EX, $550.00; Bell, "Enjoy Coca-Cola," 1970s, $3.00. Mitchell Collection

Flare, modified, "Coca-Cola," 1926, EX, $125.00; Bell with trademark in tail of C, 1930–40s, $40.00; Flare with syrup line, "Drink Coca-Cola," 1910s, EX, $400.00. Mitchell Collection

Bell, "Drink Coca-Cola," 1940–60s, $5.00. Mitchell Collection

Glass holder, "Coca-Cola," new, EX, $25.00. Mitchell Collection

Glass holder, silver, 1900, VG, $1300.00. Beware: reproductions exist. Gary Metz

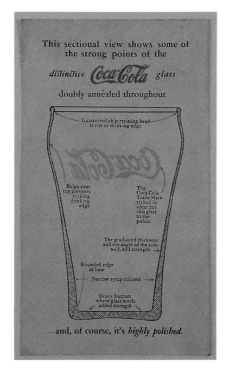

Information paper showing all the strong points of the glass, VG, $15.00. Mitchell Collection

Pewter, bell shaped, scarce, 1930s, EX, $300.00. Gary Metz

Pewter, "Coca-Cola," with original leather pouch, 1930s, EX. $750.00

**"Drink Coca-Cola Good with food,"
Wellsville China Co, 1940–50s, 7½", VG,
$750.00.** Gary Metz

**Creamer, "Drink Coca-Cola," 1930s, VG, $300.00; Sugar bowl
complete with lid,"Drink Coca-Cola," 1930, M, $350.00.** Mitchell
Collection

**Sandwich plate, "Drink Coca-Cola
Refresh yourself," 1930s, 8¼", NM,
$1,200.00.** Gary Metz

**Dish, square, "Coca-Cola" world, 1960s, 11½"x11½", EX,
$125.00.** Mitchell Collection

**Sandwich plate,
"Drink Coca-
Cola Refresh
Yourself,"
Knowles China
Co., 1931, NM,
$375.00.** Gary
Metz

Dish, round, world, 1967, 7", EX $100.00

Display bottle with original tin lid, 1923 bottle, 20" . $260.00

Pitcher, red lettered "Coca-Cola" on glass, M $55.00

Plate, Swedish, 1969, 8¼"x6¼", EX. $100.00

Art Plates

Dark headed woman facing forward with her head slightly to the left and looking upward, 10", EX, $375.00.

Western Coca-Cola™ Bottling Co, featuring a dark haired woman turned at an angle to the plate, 1908, 10" dia, EX, $350.00.

Western Coca-Cola™ Bottling Co, featuring brunette with red hair scarf holding a pink rose, 1908–12, EX, $350.00.

Western Coca-Cola™ Bottling Co, featuring dark haired woman with yellow head piece, 1908–12, 10" dia, EX, $350.00.

Western Coca-Cola™ Bottling Co, featuring dark haired woman with low drape across shoulders, 1908, 10" dia, EX, $350.00.

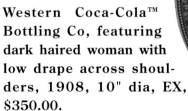

Western Coca-Cola™ Bottling Co, featuring long haired woman body forward with head and eyes to the left wearing a white drape covering off the shoulders, 1908–12, EX, $450.00.

Western Coca-Cola™ Bottling Co, featuring woman with auburn colored hair with a red adornment on the right side of her head, 1908, 10" dia, EX, $350.00.

Western Coca-Cola™ Bottling Co, featuring woman with long red hair and off the shoulder apparel, 1908–12, 10" dia, EX, $300.00.

Western Coca-Cola™ Bottling Co, profile of dark haired woman with red head piece and yellow blouse, 1908–12, 10", EX, $350.00.

Western Coca-Cola™ Bottling Co, if any art plate is in its original shadow box frame value can be doubled, 1908–12, EX, $500.00. Mitchell Collection

Glass, Silhouette Girl, with ther-mometer, 1939, 10"x14¼", VG, $850.00. Gary Metz

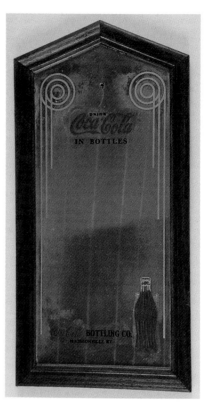

"Drink Coca-Cola in Bottles," Coca-Cola Bottling Co, Madisonville, Ky, 1920–30s, 8"x17½", $500.00. Mitchell Collection

Celluloid and metal, "Drink Coca-Cola 5¢," 1914, 1¾"x2¾", EX $600.00

Celluloid and metal, "Drink Coca-Cola," 1908, 1¾"x2¾", EX. Beware: Reproductions exist $1,100.00

Celluloid and metal, "Drink Coca-Cola," Elaine, 1916, 1¾"x2¾", EX $550.00

Celluloid and metal, "Drink Coca-Cola," Golden Girl, 1920, 1¾"x2¾", EX. Beware: Reproductions exist $700.00

Celluloid and metal, "Drink Delicious Coca-Cola" with the Coca-Cola girl, 1911, 1¾"x2¾", Hamilton King, EX. Beware: Reproductions exist $550.00

Celluloid and metal, girl on beach beside parasol, much sought after piece, 1922, 1¾"x2¾", EX. $1,750.00

Celluloid and metal, Juanita, 1906, 1¾"x2¾", EX. Beware: Reproductions exist $600.00

Celluloid and metal, "Relieves Fatigue," 1907, 1¾"x1¾", EX. $600.00

Celluloid and metal, St. Louis Fair, 1909, 1¾"x2¾", EX. Beware: Reproductions exist $600.00

Celluloid and metal, the Coca-Cola Girl, 1910, 1¾"x2¾", Hamilton King, EX. $550.00

In frame under glass "Drink Coca-Cola in Bottles Delicious Refreshing," 1930s, 8"x12", EX. $130.00

Pemberton and Chandler with ceramic dispenser in center, 1977, M $25.00

Pocket, "Coca-Cola Memos, 50th Anniversary, 1886–1936," 1936, EX $200.00

Pocket, "Coca-Cola Memos, Delicious and Refreshing," 1936, EX $200.00

Pocket, folding cardboard cat's head, "Drink Coca-Cola in bottles" on inside cover, 1920, EX, $750.00. Mitchell Collection

Pocket, "Wherever you go you will find Coca-Cola at all fountains 5¢," 1900s, G, $900.00. Mitchell Collection

Thermometers

Cardboard pre-mix counter unit thermometer with mercury scale on left then comparison chart of thermometer reading to regulator setting right, 1960s, VG, $55.00. Mitchell Collection

"Drink Coca-Cola, Delicious and Refreshing," Silhouette Girl, 1930s, 6½"x16", EX, $375.00. Mitchell Collection

Embossed die cut with 1923 Christmas bottle, 1931, VG, $200.00. Gary Metz

Desk free-standing in leather case with a round dial, hard to find, 1930s, 3¼"x3¼", EX. $1,500.00

Dial, with gold bottle outline on red center button, black numbers on face, 1908, 12" dia, NM $375.00

Metal and plastic 12" Pam style with bottle outline in center on red background, outside circle is in green with black numbers, 1950s, $425.00. Gary Metz

Metal and plastic, "Drink Coca-Cola, Sign of Good Taste," Robertson, 1950s, 12" dia, EX, $130.00. Mitchell Collection

Masonite, "Thirst knows no season," 1940s, 6¾"x17", EX, $350.00. Mitchell Collection

Metal, "Drink Coca-Cola in Bottles, Quality Refreshment," features button at top, 1950s, EX, $125.00. Mitchell Collection

Metal bottle, 1953, 17" tall, EX, $90.00. Gary Metz

Metal, gold version double bottle, "Drink Coca-Cola," metal composition, 1942, 7"x16", EX, $350.00. Mitchell Collection

Leather front, self standing desk, 1930s, 3¼"x3¼", EX $1,600.00

Liquid crystal readout design showing temp in both celsius and fahrenheit, scarce, 1970s, 10¼" sq, NM $120.00

Metal and plastic, Pam, "Drink Coca-Cola Be Really Refreshed," with fishtail, 1960s, 12" dia $500.00

Metal framed mirror with thermometer on left side and Silhouette Girl across bottom, 1930s, EX $450.00

Metal, round, "Enjoy Coca-Cola," white on red, EX . . $95.00

Metal, round, "Things Go Better With Coke," red on white, 1960s, EX $160.00

Porcelain, Canadian, Silhouette Girl, with yellow and green background, M, $1,700.00. Gary Metz

Porcelain, French, Silhouette Girl, with green and yellow background, VG, $240.00. Gary Metz

Porcelain, Canadian, Silhouette Girl, with red and yellow background, 1942, VG, $400.00. Gary Metz

Metal, stand-up, calculated in Celsius and Fahrenheit, 1940s, VG, $15.00. Mitchell Collection

Oval, Christmas bottle, 1938, 6¾"x16", EX, $225.00. Mitchell Collection

Metal, "Things go better with Coke," 1960, 12", M . $110.00

Plastic and metal, round, "Drink Coca-Cola," fishtail with green on white, 1960s, NM. $375.00

Plastic and metal, round, "Drink Coca-Cola in Bottles," white on red, VG $110.00

Porcelain, all red, French version of the Silhouette Girl, 1939, 5½"x18", M. $525.00

Porcelain, Silhouette Girl, red and green version, 1939, 5½"x18", EX $625.00

Porcelain, "Thirst Knows No Season," green background with red dot at top and Silhouette Girl at bottom, 1939, 18", EX. $600.00

Round, "Drink Coca-Cola," "Be Really Refreshed!," with fishtail logo, 1960s, 12" dia, NM. $475.00

Porcelain, French, Silhouette Girl, with red and yellow background, G, $230.00. Gary Metz

Tin, "Drink Coca-Cola in Bottles" Phone 612, Dyersburg, Tenn, with minder notations for oil, grease, and battery, 1940s, VG, $25.00. Mitchell Collection

Wooden, "Coca-Cola 5¢," 1905, F, $250.00. Mitchell Collection

Tin, bottle embossed die cut, 1933, G, $110.00. Gary Metz

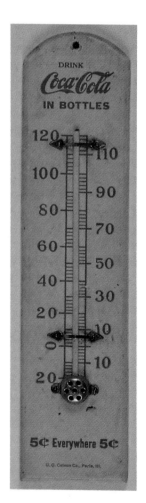

Wooden, "Drink Coca-Cola in Bottles 5¢ Everywhere," V. O. Colson Co, Paris Ill, 1910s, VG, $650.00. Mitchell Collection

Round, "Drink Coca-Cola In bottles," white on red with glass face, 1950s, 12", NM. $225.00

Round, "Drink Coca-Cola, Sign of Good Taste," 1957, 12" dia, NM $155.00

Tin, "Coke Refreshes," white on red, 1950, 8"x36", NM. $2,600.00

Tin, double bottle, 1941, VG. $300.00

Tin, embossed bottle, 1936, G $160.00

Aluminum six pack carrier with separated bottle compartments, "Coca-Cola" is embossed on side, 1940–50s, EX, $85.00. Mitchell Collection

Aluminum six pack carrier with wood and wire handle, red lettered "Drink Coca-Cola," 1950s, EX, $75.00. Mitchell Collection

Aluminum six pack king size carrier with wire handle, red lettered "Drink Coca-Cola" and "King Size," 1950, EX, $75.00. Mitchell Collection

Aluminum six pack with wire handle, separated bottle compartments, "Delicious Refreshing Coca-Cola" in white on red center panel, 1950s, EX, $45.00.
Mitchell Collection

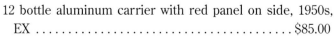

12 bottle aluminum carrier with red panel on side, 1950s, EX $85.00

24 bottle display case, 1950s, VG $170.00

48 bottle wooden shipping crate, 1910s, 9"x18"x25", VG $350.00

Bent wood with rounded corners and flat wood handle, 1940s, VG, $100.00. Mitchell Collection

Cardboard display rack, "Drink Coca-Cola Take Home a Carton," 1930s, VG, $725.00. Gary Metz

Cardboard, showing "Season's Greetings" and holly leaves, 1930s, VG, $35.00. Mitchell Collection

Cardboard six pack, red background, 1930s, EX, $100.00. Mitchell Collection

Cardboard six pack, "Serve Ice Cold," 1930s, EX, $85.00. Mitchell Collection

Cardboard, 24 bottle case, 1950s, EX $35.00

Cardboard, car window holder, 1950s, red and white, EX $25.00

Cardboard, red and white, will hold four Family Size bottles, NOS, 1958, NM $6.00

Cardboard, six bottle, bracket on end, 1924, red and green in white, EX. $250.00

Cardboard, six bottle carrier for King Size, red, white, and light green, NOS, 1960s, NM $6.00

Cardboard, six pack "Money back bottles return for deposit," dynamic wave logo, red and white, NOS, 1970s, EX $4.00

Cardboard, triangle shaped, NOS, 1950s, M $55.00

Cardboard, twelve bottle, white lettering on red background, 1950s, EX $12.00

Cardboard, twelve bottles, "Coca-Cola" in script, white on red, NOS, 1951, EX $15.00

Cardboard, twelve regular size bottles, yellow on red, 1950s, EX. $12.00

Cardboard with metal handles, "Drink Coca-Cola" on front, "Have a Coke" "Picnic Cooler" on sides, red with white lettering, 1956, EX, $130.00.
Mitchell Collection

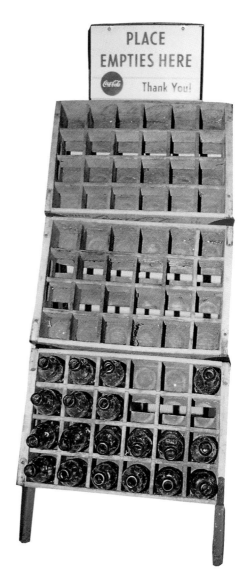

Metal three case bottle rack with "Place Empties Here, Thank You" sign at top, red, G, $125.00. Mike and Debbie Summers

Metal grocery cart two bottle holder with sign on front "Enjoy Coca-Cola while you shop, Place Bottles Here," 1950s, EX, $35.00. Mitchell Collection

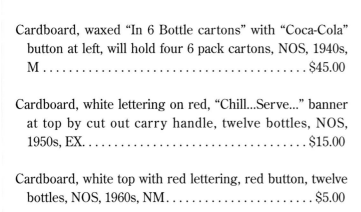

Cardboard, waxed "In 6 Bottle cartons" with "Coca-Cola" button at left, will hold four 6 pack cartons, NOS, 1940s, M $45.00

Cardboard, white lettering on red, "Chill...Serve..." banner at top by cut out carry handle, twelve bottles, NOS, 1950s, EX. $15.00

Cardboard, white top with red lettering, red button, twelve bottles, NOS, 1960s, NM. $5.00

Cardboard with top carrying handle, will hold six bottles, "Drink Coca-Cola Delicious and Refreshing," "Serve Ice Cold," 1929, EX. $75.00

Cardboard with wire handle, white lettering on red, six bottle, NOS, 1950s, NM $45.00

Display case for giant 20" bottles, 1950s, VG $180.00

Masonite six pack carrier, 1940s, EX $65.00

Metal and wire 18 bottle, Canadian, 1930–1940, red, VG $275.00

Glassrock salesman's sample, complete with under cooler case storage metal, NM, $1,000.00. Mitchell Collection

Vendo coin changer with keys, reproduction sign, EX, $625.00. Gary Metz

Vendo V-81, much sought after for home use due to its compact design and ability to dispense different size bottles, 1950s, 27"x58"x16", white on red, VG, $500.00. Mike and Debbie Summers

Jacobs vending machine model #26, upright shaped like a mailbox, very sought after but also the most common of Jacobs machines, 1940–50s, red, EX. $1,100.00

Vendo coin changer with keys and "Have a Coke" sign under glass, 12"x15" $625.00

Vendo V-23, box cooler that will vend 23 bottles, made in a standard and deluxe version, fairly easy to find, 1940–50s, red and silver, EX $400.00

Vendo V-44, an upright box that is highly sought after by collectors, will dispense 44 bottles, 1950s, red and white, EX $1,600.00

Vendo V-56, upright, will dispense 56 bottles, 1950s, red and white, EX $700.00

Vendo V-59 top chest cooler electric, dispense 59 bottles, not very sought after by collectors, 1940s, red, EX. . . . $150.00

Vendo V-80, upright, will dispense 80 bottles, not aggressively sought after so still relatively easy to find and easy to buy, 1950s, red and white, EX $450.00

Vendo V-81, dispenses 81 bottles, upright, this machine is also sought after by collectors but is still fairly easy to find, 1950s, red and white, EX $750.00

Vendo V-83, dispenses 83 bottles, very common, 1940–50, red, EX $200.00

Westinghouse salesman's sample metal two door lift up cooler, EX, $800.00. Mitchell Collection

Victor C-45A salesman's sample chest cooler, cardboard, 1940–50s, G, $100.00. Mitchell Collection

Vendolator 27, known as the table top, this machine would set on a desk or special stand, dispenses 27 bottles, still fairly easy to find, 1940s, 24"x27"x19", red, EX .. $850.00

Vendolator 33, upright that dispenses 33 bottles, relative common, 1950s, red, EX $500.00

Vendolator 44, upright that dispenses 44 bottles, not hard to find, 1950s, red and white, EX. $1,200.00

Vendolator 72, upright will dispense 72 bottles, will only serve 6½ oz. bottles, 1950s, red, EX $550.00

Vendor V-39, box type cooler that will vend 39 bottles and will pre-cool slightly more than this number, 1940s, red, EX $550.00

Westinghouse 3 Case Junior electric chest box, dispenses 75 bottles, 1940–50s, red, EX $375.00

Westinghouse 3 Case Junior, ice cooled chest box, 1940–50s, red, EX. $425.00

Westinghouse 6 Case Master dispenses 140 bottles, chest box electric, 1940s, red and stainless steel, EX .. $300.00

Westinghouse 6 Case Master wet chest type box dispenses 144 bottles, 1940s, red, EX $375.00

Westinghouse salesman's sample standard, box, metal, EX, $900.00. Mitchell Collection

Westinghouse Master electric chest cooler, dispenses 144 bottles fairly common, 1930–40, red, EX. $300.00

Westinghouse Standard ice chest, dispenses 102 bottles, 1930s, red, EX. $250.00

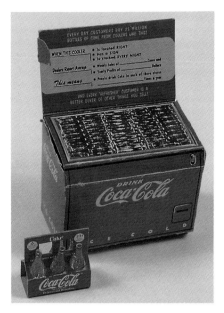

Westinghouse WE-6, salesman's sample, 1940–50s, 4⅜x4"x3", G, $100.00. Mitchell Collection

Zinc lined wet box for cooling and dispensing, "Help Yourself Drink Coca-Cola Deposit in Box 5¢," wood exterior, 1920s, $310.00. Gary Metz

Coolers

Ball park vendor complete with canvas straps and opener, has divider and is insulated, 1940s – 50s, VG, $200.00. Mitchell Collection

Airline, stainless steel, 1950s, 12"x17"x7", NM . . . $1,700.00

Airline, with top handle, 1950s, red, NM $450.00

Aluminum, 12 pack, 1950s, 12 pack, EX $85.00

Dispenser, refills from top, red metal with cream lettering, 1950s, VG $325.00

Floor chest, embossed lettering, yellow and white lettering on red background with bottle at left side, 29"x32½"hx22"d, VG, $950.00. Gary Metz

Dispenser, fountain, red with white lettering, 1940s, EX $325.00

Dispenser, soda fountain, red and white, 1940–50s, EX. $675.00

Salesman's sample sale aid shaped like box cooler, EX, $85.00. Mitchell Collection

Salesman's sample counter dispenser with original carrying case and complete presentation unit, light inside lights up glasses, very rare, 1960s, 4½"wx6½"dx6¾", EX, $2,500.00. Gary Metz

Metal picnic, small, "Drink Coca-Cola in Bottles," 1950s, VG, $130.00. Mitchell Collection

Dispenser, soda fountain, red sides with chrome lid, two tops, 1930s, EX $675.00

Floor, large, resembling a large picnic cooler, 1950s, red, NM $3,000.00

Hemp Model 9022 picnic, white "Drink" on red, metal latch and handle, NOS, 1950s, M $500.00

Metal picnic, with bottle in hand decal, 1940–50s, 13"x12"x8", EX $110.00

Stadium vendor, "Have a Coke," 16"x10"x21", $50.00. Gary Metz

Vinyl picnic with fishtail logo, shaped like a box with a fold over top and strap "Refreshing New Feeling," NM. $45.00

Radios

Can with the dynamic wave, 1970s, EX, $45.00. Mitchell Collection

Bottle shaped, AM/FM, plastic, 1970s, EX, $35.00. Mitchell Collection

Cooler design, upright, 1960s, G, $165.00. Mitchell Collection

Cooler design, upright, 1980s, EX, $75.00. Mitchell Collection

Cooler design, upright, J. Russell, 1970s, EX, $110.00. Mitchell Collection

Cooler shaped crystal with ear piece, if all parts including instructions are present increase price to $200.00, EX, $175.00. Mitchell Collection

Bottle shaped, 1933, VG. . . . . $3,300.00   Cooler, lights up and plays, 1950s, EX. $900.00

Cooler design, upright, with dynamic wave, 1970s, EX, $125.00. Mitchell Collection

Cooler, upright, 1950s, F, $200.00. Mitchell Collection

Cooler, prices on these vary greatly, some will go into the thousands, while others fall below the book price, remember condition, 1950s, red, VG, $625.00. Gary Metz

Clocks

Boudoir, leather with gold logo at bottom, "Drink Coca-Cola So Easily Served," 1910, 3"x8", $1,300.00. Gary Metz

Anniversary style dome, 1950s, 3"x5", EX, $750.00. Mitchell Collection

Counter, "Drink Coca-Cola Please Pay When Served," yellow numbers on black background, 19¼"x9", VG, $400.00.

Gilbert key wound case, "Drink Coca-Cola" in red lettering on white clock face, "In Bottles 5¢" on pendulum door glass, 1916-20s, EX, $1,300.00. Beware: Reproductions exist.

Desk, leather composition with "Drink Coca-Cola in Bottles 5¢" at top center over clock works and smaller bottles at hour right and left hand corners, 1910, 4⅓"x6", EX, $1,100.00.

"Drink Coca-Cola 5¢ Delicious, Refreshing 5¢," Baird Clock Co, 15 day movement, working, 1896–99, EX, $6,500.00.

Dome, white lettering "Drink Coca-Cola" in red center, 1950s, 6"x9", EX $1,000.00

"Drink Coca-Cola in Bottles," wooden frame, 1939–40, 16"x16", G, $175.00. Gary Metz

Gilbert pendulum with original finish, 1930s, VG, $1,200.00. Gary Metz

Gilbert case, "Drink Coca-Cola" in red lettering on clock face and decal of girl with a bottle on bottom glass door, 1910, 18"x40", EX, $4,500.00.

Gilbert regulator with Gibson girl decal on glass, 1910, EX, $6,000.00. Gary Metz

Celluloid desk, Hilda Clark seated at table holding a glass in a holder, clock is in lower left portion of piece, working, rare and hard to find, 1901, 5½"x7¾", EX, $8,500.00.

"Drink Coca-Cola" red and white plastic, round, EX, $450.00. Mitchell Collection

Electric, plastic white background, 1970s, EX $65.00

Light-up neon counter, "Pause Drink Coca-Cola," showing bottle spotlighted, restored, rare, and hard to find piece, 1930s, EX, $4,500.00. Mitchell Collection

Light-up counter top clock and sign, restored, 1950, $525.00.
Gary Metz

Ingraham with restored regulator on bottom glass, some fade in to clock face, 1905, VG, $950.00. Gary Metz

Light-up advertising by Modern Clock Advertising Company in Brooklyn N.Y, aluminum case with plastic face, 1950s, 24" dia, red on white, VG $300.00

Light-up, "Drink Coca-Cola in Bottles," button in center with white on red, numbers are black on white, by Swilhart, 1950s, 15" dia, EX $375.00

Light-up fish tail with green background, "Drink Coca-Cola" in white lettering on red fishtail background, 1960s, EX. $150.00

Light-up fishtail with white background, 1960, EX . $145.00

Light-up round with "Drink Coca-Cola" in red on white background with bottle above number 6, 1950s, VG $400.00

Light-up counter top, "Serve Yourself," 1940 – 50s, EX $750.00

Light-up fishtail clock, NOS, 1960s, EX, $240.00. Gary Metz

Maroon, on wings, 1950s, 17½" dia, EX, $250.00.

Neon, octagonal, "Ice Cold Coca-Cola," Silhouette Girl, 1940s, 18", VG, $1,600.00. Gary Metz

Left: Plastic pocket watch, 1970s, EX, $35.00. Right: Pocket watch, with second hand dial at bottom, VG, $75.00. Mitchell Collection

Maroon, on wings with Sprite Boy on each end, it's hard to find these with wings still attached, even harder to find them with the Sprite Boy on the ends, 1950s, 17½" w/o wings, EX $850.00

Metal and plastic construction dot logo at 4 and 5, "Things Go Better With Coke" where 10 and 11 should be, 16"x16", EX $75.00

Metal framed electric with silhouette girl above number 6, 1930–40, 18" dia, EX. $800.00

Metal framed glass front by Lackner, has bottle in circle at top of number 6, 1940s, 16"x16", M $950.00

Neon, bottle on octagon with logo, metal case with yellow border, 1942, 16"x16", EX $900.00

Neon, octagonal, featuring Silhouette Girl logo on center disc, "Ice Cola Cola Coca-Cola," 1941, EX $1,450.00

Plastic and metal, "Things go better with Coke," 16"x16", EX, $60.00.

Wall, spring driven pendulum, "Coca-Cola, The Ideal Brain Tonic," Baird Clock Co, 1891–95, 24" tall, EX, $5,000.00.

Round Silhouette Girl with metal frame, 1930 – 40s, 18" dia, VG, $750.00. Mitchell Collection

Travel, German made with brass case, 1960s, 3"x3", $120.00. Mitchell Collection

Telechron, red dot in hour position with white background and white wings, 1948, 36" wing span, VG, $450.00. Mitchell Collection

Neon, octagonal, with Silhouette Girl above number, 1930s, EX. Beware: Reproduction exist $1,200.00

Neon surrounded by rainbow banner from 9 to 3, "Drink Coca-Cola-Sign of Good Taste" on rainbow panel, 1950s, 24" dia, NM $2,700.00

Plastic body electric with fake pendulum and a light-up base with "Coca-Cola" in base, 1970s, G $45.00

Plastic body, white background with red lettering and "Coca-Cola" written in lower right hand corner, 1960s, 16"x16", EX. $125.00

Plastic pocket watch shape, "Drink Coca-Cola," 18" dia, EX. $45.00

Reproduction Betty, 1974, VG $50.00

Reproduction plastic regulator style, 1972, EX. $50.00

Round, pulsating Silhouette Girl, cut number 6 on dial, fairly rare, 1930s, 18" dia, EX. $2,900.00

Wood framed with "Drink Coca-Cola in Bottles" in white on red background, 1930s, 16"x16", EX $400.00

Wood framed with Silhouette Girl at bottom center, 1930s, 16"x16", EX. $850.00

Wooden regulator, pendulum, oak case, key wound "Drink Coca-Cola In Bottles" in black on white face, 1980s, 23"h, M $150.00

Top row: Formed hand, many versions, ca. 1940s, $20.00; formed hand, many versions, ca. 1920s, $25.00; formed hand, poor condition, ca. 1940s, $5.00. Second row: ca. 1940s, $25.00; formed hand version, ca. 1950s, $15.00; can piercer, metal, "... Coke," ca. 1970s, $10.00. Third row: combination can and bottle, 1980s, $8.00; plastic handle can piercer and cap opener, ca. 1950s – 70s, $8.00. Fourth row: 50th Anniversary, 1950s, EX, $55.00; Spoon opener, 1920–30, 7½", EX, $75.00. Bottom: plastic handle with dynamic wave, 1960s, $8.00; metal, "Drink Coca-Cola," $5.00. Mitchell Collection

Top: "Drink Coca-Cola," plastic and metal, red and white, EX, $3.00. Bottom: 75th Anniversary from Columbus Ohio, plastic and metal, 1970s, EX, $15.00. Mitchell Collection

Bakelite and metal, 1950s, black, EX, $55.00. Chief Paduke Antiques

Bottle stopper and opener, "Glascock Bros. Mfg. Co, Coca-Cola Quality Coolers," 1919–20s, EX, $85.00. Antiques Cards, Collectibles

Bottle shaped, 1950s, EX, $100.00.

Bottle shaped, EX, $20.00. Mitchell Collection

Card suit, stainless steel set in marked carrier sleeves, 1970s, EX. $45.00

"Coca-Cola" block print cast iron wishbone, 1900s, EX, $115.00.

Top, from left: Corkscrew, wall mounted, 1920s, EX, $75.00; Corkscrew, wall mounted, 1950s, EX, $35.00; Cast "Drink Coca-Cola" wall mount, 1930s, EX, $10.00. Center: Wall mounted metal "Drink Coca-Cola," also has been referred to as bent metal opener, 1950, EX, $20.00. Bottom: Opener, formed hand version, several versions exist, ca. 1930s, $25.00; Opener, over the top "Drink Coca-Cola," several version, ca. 1940s, $25.00. Mitchell Collection

"Coca-Cola Bottles" key style, 1930s, EX, $45.00.

"Drink Bottled Coca-Cola" saber shaped opener, 1920s, EX, $200.00.

"Drink Coca-Cola™ in Bottles," 1920–40s, EX, $20.00.

"Drink Coca-Cola in Bottles" brass key, 1910s, EX, $100.00.

"Drink Coca-Cola™ in Sterilized Bottles" lollipop shaped, 1930s, EX, $85.00.

"Drink Coca-Cola" key shaped with bottle cap facsimile at top, 1920–50s, EX, $35.00.

Cigar box cutter "Delicious & Refreshing," 1905 – 15, EX. $85.00

"Drink Coca-Cola™," straight, 1910 – 50s, EX, $20.00.

Flat metal, 1950s, EX, $35.00.

"Have a Coke.™," 1950–60s, EX, $5.00.

"Have A Coke," wire, EX, $3.00.

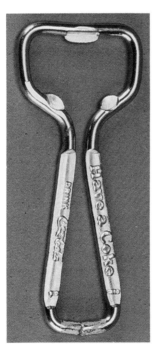

Metal, closely resembling leg, 1920, EX, $200.00.

"Have a Coke" beer type, $5.00.

Rail puller and crate opener from Piqua Coca-Cola Bottling Co, 1960s, EX, $85.00. Mitchell Collection

Fish tail spinner, 1910–30, EX $150.00

Hand spinner, "You Pay," 1910–20, EX $120.00

Metal, eagle head, "Drink Coca-Cola," engraved, 1919–20s, EX $165.00

Metal lion head, 1910–30s, EX $160.00

Metal, logo at end with "Drink Bottled Coca-Cola," hard to find, 1908, EX $160.00

Metal with a solid handle, "Shirts For the Coke Set," EX $20.00

Opener and spoon combination, 1930s, EX . . . . $125.00.

Steel, black with red background, outing style, 1910–20s, EX $100.00

Turtle style with four devices, "Drink Coca-Cola in Bottles," 1970s, EX $12.00

Nashville, Tenn, celebrating 50th Anniversary, metal, gold plated bottle shaped with opener at bottom of bottle, 1952, EX, $75.00.

Starr "X" wall mount in original box, 1940–1980, EX, $5.00.

Knives

Top: One blade and one opener, "Coca-Cola Bottling Company," 1910s, EX, $225.00. Bottom: "The Coca-Cola Bottling Co." blade has to be marked Kaster & Co. Coca-Cola Bottling Co, Germany, 1905–15, brass, EX, $400.00. Beware: Reproduction exist. Mitchell Collection

Bone handle combination knife and opener, red lettering, "Drink Coca-Cola in Bottles," 1915–25, EX $125.00

Bone handle, two blade, "Delicious and Refreshing," 1920, VG $100.00

Pearl handle with corkscrew blade and opener, 1930s, EX, $110.00. Mitchell Collection

Combination Henry Sears & Son, Solingen, one blade with case shaped like boot as opener, "Coca-Cola," 1920s, white, EX $400.00

"Compliments - The Coca-Cola™ Co," 1930s, EX. . . . $75.00

"Drink Coca-Cola™ in Bottles," 1940s, EX $75.00

Pearl handle, "Serve Coca-Cola™," 1940s, EX $175.00

Switchblade, Remington, "Drink Coca-Cola in Bottles," 1930s, EX. $225.00

"The Coca-Cola™ Bottling Co" embossed on side, 1940s, EX $45.00

Truck shaped from seminar, 1972, EX $12.00

"When Thirsty Try A Bottle" embossed on side with bottle, 1910, EX $350.00

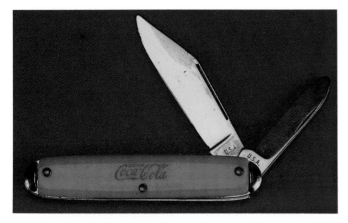

Two blade, "Drink Coca-Cola," $35.00.

Stainless steel with one blade and nail file, 1950–60s, EX, $30.00. Mitchell Collection

Two blade pen knife, "Enjoy Coca-Cola," all metal, EX, $15.00.

Small metal utility with a cutting blade, an opener, and a nail file with key chain, "Enjoy Coca-Cola," EX, $12.00.

Ice Picks

Bulb type handle, large, 1920s, VG, $60.00. Mitchell Collection

Ice pick and bottle opener, 1920s, VG, $45.00. Mitchell Collection

Squared wooden handle advertising "Coca-Cola in Bottles" and "Ice-Coal Phone 87," 1930–40s, EX, $25.00. Mitchell Collection

Wooden handle, 1960s, EX, $10.00. Mitchell Collection

Wooden handle, bottle opener in the handle end, 1930, EX, $40.00. Mitchell Collection

Ashtrays

Glass from Dickson, Tennessee, EX, $15.00. Mitchell Collection

Left: Top match pull Bakelite, rare, 1940s, EX, $700.00. Right: Bottle lighter, 1950s, EX, $100.00. Mitchell Collection

"High in energy, Low in calories," tin, 1950s, EX, $20.00. Mitchell Collection

Bronze colored, depicting 50th Anniversary in center, 1950s, EX, $55.00. Mitchell Collection

Bottle, 1950s, EX $125.00

"Drink Coca-Cola™," round with scalloped edge, 1950s, EX. $8.00

"Drink Coca-Cola™," round, 1960, EX $5.00

"Support Your Fireman, Compliments of Coca-Cola," tin rectangular, EX. $225.00

Metal with molded cigarette holder, EX, $20.00. Mitchell Collection

"The pause that refreshes & J.J. Flynn Co," square glass, red round center, 1950s, EX $65.00

"Things go Better with Coke™," square metal, 1960s, red, EX $8.00

Wave logo from Mexico, 1970s, EX, $3.00.

Set of four, ruby red, price should be doubled if set is in original box, 1950s, EX, $350.00. Mitchell Collection

Lighters

"Drink Coca-Cola," 1950s, EX, $25.00. Mitchell Collection

Dispose-a-lite in original box, 1970s, EX $15.00

"Enjoy Coca-Cola" on bottom, flip top, gold plate, NM . $85.00

Executive award, 1984, NM $25.00

Gold Sygnus standup, 1962, EX $140.00

Musical, red "Drink" on white dot, EX $155.00

Red lettering on the diagonal with gold-tone background, 1962, EX $135.00

Silver with embossed bottle, flip top, M $35.00

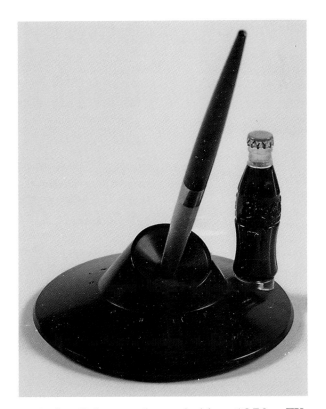

Bakelite lighter and pen holder, 1950s, EX, $130.00. Mitchell Collection

From left: Musical, 1970s, EX, $200.00; Round with diamond shaped pattern, "Enjoy Coca-Cola," 1960s, $35.00; Can-shaped, with dynamic wave, M, $30.00; Bottle-shaped, fairly common, without the lighter it's known as "the pill box," 1950, M, $20.00. Mitchell Collection

Matches

Book, 50th Anniversary, 1936, EX, $8.00. Mitchell Collection

Book, "A Distinctive Drink in a Distinctive Bottle," 1922, EX, $100.00. Mitchell Collection

Book, "Have a Coke," 1950s, VG, $5.00. Mitchell Collection

Top: Book from 1982 World's Fair at Knoxville, Tenn, 1982, EX, $1.00. Bottom: Book from New York World's Fair, 1964, $8.00. Mitchell Collection

Left: Book, "King Size Coke," 1959, VG, $4.00. Right: Book, "Vote for A. A. Nelson, Railroad Commissioner," VG, $3.00. Mitchell Collection

Book, "Have a Coke," bottle in hand, 1940–50s, VG, $4.00. Mitchell Collection

Book with bottle on cover, 1910–20s, VG $750.00

Left: Book for Westinghouse coolers for the Bottlers of Coca-Cola, G, $2.00. Right: Book from the Coca-Cola Bottling Co. at Fulton, Ky, Telephone 447, EX, $2.00. Mitchell Collection

Matchbook holder with matches, metal, 1959, EX, $110.00.

Mitchell Collection

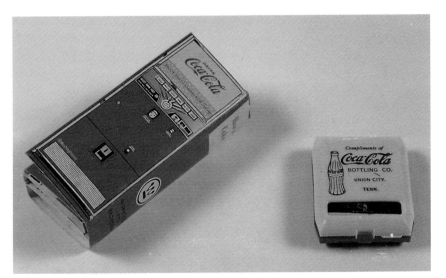

Left: Book, is make up of Westinghouse cooler, $30.00. Right: Safe & strikes, 1930s, EX, $250.00. Mitchell Collection

Book with woman on front, 1910s, VG $950.00

Match strikes, porcelain, French, NM $250.00

Matchbook holder, celluloid, 1910, EX $300.00

Matchbook holder, "Compliments of The Coca-Cola Co. Coca-Cola Relieves Fatigue," 1907, EX $300.00

Matchbook holder, "Drink Coca-Cola at Soda Fountains 5¢," 1907, EX. $350.00

Safe, "Drink Coca-Cola in Bottles," 1908, EX $600.00

Striker, "Drink Coca-Cola, Strike Matches Here" beginning to be a scarce item, 1939, red, white, yellow $400.00

Holder, tin, "Drink Coca-Cola in Bottles," 1940s, F, $350.00.

Mitchell Collection

Striker, porcelain, "Drink Coca-Cola Strike Matches here," English, yellow and white lettering with red background and black match strike field, NM $500.00

Coasters

Clockwise, from top: Metal with Santa Claus, white, $5.00; Plastic with dynamic wave, "Enjoy Coca-Cola," red, EX, 1970s, $5.00; Aluminum, 1960s, green, EX, $4.00; Metal, "Drink Coca-Cola," EX, $5.00; Metal, Hilda Clark artwork, EX, $5.00; Metal with Juanita, 1984, EX, $5.00. Center: Cardboard, "Go with Coke," 1960s, red and white, EX, $5.00. Mitchell Collection

Clockwise from top: Foil showing lady with a bottle, square, M, $5.00; Foil showing a street car scene, M, $5.00; Foil showing party tray and cooler, square, M, $5.00; Foil showing hand in bottle with world globe behind square, M, $5.00. Mitchell Collection

Paper program for the 37th National Convention in Miami, Fla. Oct. 10, 11, 12, 13 (55), American Legion, Drink Coca-Cola, 1955, VG, $30.00. Mitchell Collection

"Drink Coca-Cola ice cold," with Silhouette Girl, 1940s, M $12.00

"Have a Coke" with Sprite Boy, 1940s, M $8.00

Top: "Please put empties in the rack," green and white, $10.00; "Things go better with Coke," red lettering on white background, round, $5.00. Bottom: "Have a Coke" with Sprite Boy in bottle cap hat, M, $10.00; "Things go better with Coke," red and white, square with scalloped edges, M, $3.00. Mitchell Collection

No Drip Protectors

Left: Bottle bag, the distinctive Coca-Cola glass, EX, $5.00. Right: Bottle bag, used in the days of "wet" coolers to keep the customer dry, 1931, EX, $5.00. Mitchell Collection

"A Great Drink...With Good Things To Eat," 1938, NM $3.00

Bottle protector, 1948, EX. $3.00

Bottle protector, 1934, EX. $4.00

Bottle protector, 1944, EX. $3.00

Featuring a couple dancing, 1946, NM $3.00

Bottle protector, 1932, VG, $5.00. Mitchell Collection

"In Bottles" protector, 1930, NM $3.00

Paper bottle protector, 1946, EX $3.00

Rear view of man drinking from a bottle, 1936, NM . . $3.00

"The Pause That Refreshes," featuring three bottles, 1936, NM. $3.00

Menu Boards

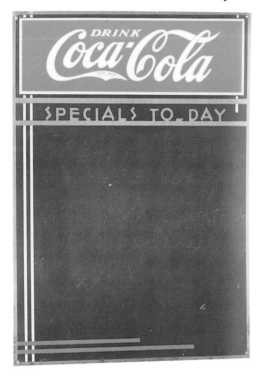

Kay Displays, wood and metal with button at center, 1930s, EX, $275.00. Gary Metz

**"Drink Coca-Cola Specials Today,"
1930s, G, $175.00.** Gary Metz

Metal and wood, "Drink Coca-Cola" in white lettering inside red fishtail on green background, metal menu strips, 1950s, VG, $125.00.

Mitchell Collection

Kay Displays, wood with metal trim, "Drink Coca-Cola," 1940s, EX, $450.00. Mitchell Collection

Cardboard stand-up, "Refreshing You Best," 1950s, EX . $110.00

Kay Displays, 1940–50s, 3'x1', NM $2,400.00

Kay Displays, "Drink" on spotlight with full glass and gold tone slots on both sides, 1940–50s, 36"x12", EX. . $475.00

Light-up design with clock, 1960s, EX. $125.00

Metal, "Drink Coca-Cola Delicious and Refreshing," Silhouette Girl in lower right corner, 1930s, VG $200.00

"Refresh Yourself" with bottle and cap lower right hand corner, 1930, 20"x28", VG $300.00

Tin, "Drink Coca-Cola" at extreme top with "Specials Today" under that and on top of blackboard section, 1934, 20"x28", VG. $350.00

Tin, "Specials Today, Coca-Cola" oval at top and bottle in lower right hand side, blackboard for easy menu changes, 1929, 20"x28", F $150.00

Wave logo at top, 1970s, 20"x28", M $30.00

Tin, die cut, "Drink Coca-Cola Be Refreshed," Canadian, 1950, EX, **$210.00.** Gary Metz

Tin, arched top embossed with fishtail design at top, NM, **$375.00.** Gary Metz

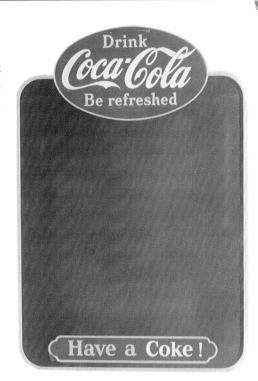

Door Pushes

"Refreshing Coca-Cola New Feelings," 1950–60s, EX, **$125.00.** Mitchell Collection

Aluminum bottle, 1930–40, NM $275.00

"Drink Coca-Cola/Ice Cold/In Bottles," porcelain, red and white lettering on red and white background, 35" long, NM. $255.00

Porcelain and wrought iron, adjustable, "Drink Coca-Cola" in center, 1930s, EX $260.00

Porcelain, "Come In! Have a Coca-Cola," yellow and white lettering on red background, 3½"x11½", NM . . . $290.00

Porcelain, horizontal, "Have a Coca-Cola," yellow and white lettering on red background trimmed in yellow, 6½"x3½" . . . $260.00

Porcelain, "Ice Cold in Bottles," red on white, 1960s, 30", EX $250.00

Porcelain, "Iced Coca-Cola Here," yellow and white lettering on red background, 1950s, 31", EX $150.00

Porcelain, oversized, outdoor style, with original box, 1942, 18"x54", NM $1,700.00

Porcelain, "Thanks Call Again For A Coca-Cola," yellow and white lettering red background, 4"x11½" . . . $210.00

Porcelain, "Thanks Call again for a Coca-Cola," yellow and white lettering on red, Canadian, 1930s, EX $200.00

Porcelain, vertical, "Thanks Call Again for a Coca-Cola," yellow and white lettering on red background, 3½"x13½", NM. $325.00

Tin, "Refresh Yourself," 1940–50, 3"x6", G $250.00

Tin, "Refresh Yourself," 1940–50, 3"x6", NM $330.00

Tin, silhouette, 1939–41, 33"x3½", EX $375.00

Porcelain and wrought iron, "Drink Coca-Cola," 1930s, EX, $425.00. Mitchell Collection

Metal and plaster, "Drink Coca-Cola Delicious Refreshing," 1930–40s, EX, $110.00. Mitchell Collection

Metal and plastic, "Have a Coke!" on door attachment, 1930, NM, $135.00. Chief Paduke Antiques Mall

Trucks

"Big Wheel," "Drink Coca-Cola," add $30.00 if MIB, 1970, EX, $50.00. Mitchell Collection

Bank, wooden van with stamped logo, driver, and cases, 1980s, 7", EX $20.00

Barclay open bed, even load, 1950, 2", yellow, EX . . $175.00

Bedford, Oinky, even load, open body, 1950s, 4½", red and white, NM $325.00

Buddy L #5646 GMC with all original accessories in box, 1957, yellow, EX, $650.00. Gary Metz

Berlist Stradair of France, 1960s, 4¼", EX $275.00

Buddy L #420C, 1978, G $20.00

Buddy L Ford with original box and all accessories, 1960s, NM, $550.00. Gary Metz

Buddy L, "Enjoy Coca-Cola," complete with hand truck that mounts in side compartment, add $15.00 if MIB, 1970, EX, $45.00. Mitchell Collection

Buddy L with cases and bottles, 1960s, EX, $250.00. Mitchell Collection

Buddy L No #5546 International in original box with all accessories, 1956, NM, $725.00. Gary Metz

Buddy L #4969, scarce tractor-trailer rig, 1970s, NM . $80.00

Buddy L #4973 set, 7 pieces, 1970s, NM $55.00

Buddy L, 5-piece set, 1981, NM $55.00

Buddy L #5215, 1970s, NM. $25.00

Buddy L #5215 H, big tires, pressed steel, 1980s, red and white, M $25.00

Buddy L #5216 plastic A-frame, will hold eight cases, in original box, 1962, yellow, EX. $375.00

Buddy L #5426, pressed steel, 1960, 15", NMIB . . . $500.00

Buddy L #5426 truck, steel, Ford style with chrome grille, 1960s, yellow, NM $110.00

Buddy L #5646, GMC loader with case loading line, 1950s, yellow $450.00

Buddy L #591-1350, steel, Japan, 1980s, 11", EX $75.00

Buddy L #666 set, 15 pieces, 1980s, M $45.00

Budgie even load, 1950, 5", yellow, EX $450.00

Chevy delivery, tin, Smokeyfest Estb. 1930, 1995, MIB. $25.00

Cargo style with working headlights and taillights, 1950, VG, $275.00. Gary Metz

Gas, made in Germany, model #426-20, a rare and desirable tin windup litho with great detailing with a full load of tin and plastic cases, 1949, yellow, EX, $2,600.00. Gary Metz

Marx #991 with gray cab and frame in original box, 1953, yellow and gray, NM, $900.00. Gary Metz

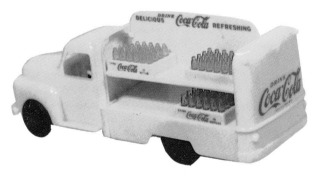

Marx Ford style, 1950s, yellow, EX, $375.00. Gary Metz

Corgi Jr. featuring contour logo, 1982, NM $18.00

Corgi, Jr. double decker bus, 1974, 3", EX $12.00

Durham Industries van in original packaging, 1970–80s, NM. $20.00

El Camino given away at convention in Ohio, plastic, 1995, red and white, MIB $15.00

Goodies van, Canadian, contour logo, 1970s, 12", M. $110.00

Lemerzarugyar plastic van, friction, 7", silver, MIB . $105.00

Lemezarugyar van, Hungary, plastic friction, 1970s, red, MIB $215.00

London, "Drink Coca-Cola" decal on side, 1960s, EX . $265.00

Marx #1090, tin, open bed, 1956, 17", yellow and red, EX $450.00

Marx #21, open divided double decker bed, 1954, 12½", yellow and red, NM $275.00

Marx #991, pressed steel, Sprite Boy decal, 1950s, gray, MIB $1000.00

Marx #991, pressed steel, Sprite Boy decal, 1950s, red and yellow, G $150.00

Marx No. 21 open side, 1950s, yellow, EX $450.00

Marx, stake, Sprite Boy, 1940s, yellow, EX. $650.00

Matchbox, tractor-trailer, Super King, 1978, NMIB. . $40.00

Marx, metal, 1950s, yellow, VG, $450.00. Mitchell Collection

Marx, stake, yellow bed with red cab and frame with Sprite Boy decal on side of bed, 1950, G, $295.00. Gary Metz

Marx plastic with original six Coca-Cola cases, Canadian, 1950s, red, EX, $525.00. Gary Metz

Matchbox with even load bed, "Drink Coca-Cola," 1960s, 2", yellow, EX $65.00

Matchbox with staggered load bed, "Drink Coca-Cola," 1960s, yellow, EX $125.00

Maxitoys brand, made of metal with rubber tires made in Holland, only 500 made so it's fairly rare, 1980s, 11", EX $475.00

Maxitoys/Holland metal van with open sided driver's seat, 1980s, 11", yellow and black, EX $275.00

Maxwell Co, plastic delivery van, India, 1970s, EX . . $45.00

Metalcraft #171 A-frame, 1932, red and yellow, EX . $900.00

Metalcraft #171 pressed steel, rubber wheels, A frame, 1932, red and yellow, NMIB. $2,500.00

Model T, cast iron, 1980s, M. Warning: Fantasy item. $10.00

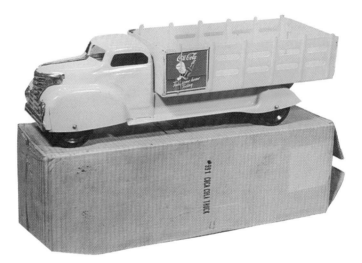

Marx No. 991 with Sprite Boy decal on side, in original box, 1951, yellow, NM, $625.00. Gary Metz

Marx, if in MIB condition with original box this value would nearly double, 1950, G, $225.00. Mitchell Collection

Model T, scale kit in original box, 1970s, MIB $55.00

Osahi, Japan, van, tin and plastic, friction, 1970s, EX . $75.00

Metalcraft with rubber tires, if this item were MIB price could go up by as much as $400.00, 1930s, G, $750.00. Mitchell Collection

Panel type, AMBO with smooth tires tin litho, 1960s, EX $550.00

Plastic Fun Mates from Straco, wind-up, 1970s, EX . $30.00

Plastic, smooth tire, 1940–50s, yellow, EX $95.00

Renault, solid metal, 1970s, yellow, NM $55.00

Renault, solid metal, 1970s, red, NM. $55.00

Rico Sanson-Junior with contour logo, 1970s, 13½", red, EX. $45.00

Rosko friction motor, beverage delivery, 1950, 8", EX. $475.00

Sanyo/A. Haddock Co route, battery operated, in original box, 1960s, yellow, white, red, EX $275.00

Siki Eurobuilt, Mack tractor trailer, die cast, 1980s, 12½", MIB $45.00

Siku-Oldtimes, metal, 1980s, 5¼", EX. $40.00

Smith-Miller A-frame, wood and aluminum, rubber tires, 1944, 14", red, EX $1,600.00

Smith-Miller, wood and metal with bottle logos on bed, 1947–53, 14", red, EX. $695.00

Smith Miller, metal, GMC number 2 of 50 stamped on bottom, with six original cases of 24 green bottles in original box, #1 is in the Smith Miller Museum, rare, 1979, red, EX, $1,700.00. Gary Metz

Straco, plastic Wee People, Hong Kong, 5½", EX . . . $40.00

Supervan, plastic, 1970s, 18"x11", NM $110.00

Tin, even load, Japanese, 1950s, 4", yellow, EX $150.00

Tin Lineman, friction power, 1950s, VG $200.00

Tin van, "Drink Coca-Cola, Delicious, Refreshing," Japanese, 1950, 4", yellow. $150.00

Tootsie Toy van copy, die cast metal, white lettering, 1986, M $12.00

Uni Plast, Mexican #302, van with contour logo, plastic, 1978–79, red, NM. $25.00

Van, cardboard, Max Headroom, 1980s, 6", NM $10.00

Winrose, Atlanta Convention, 1994, MIB $165.00

VW van with friction motor by Taiyo, 1950s, 7½"
long, VG, $225.00. Mitchell Collection

Vending machine style ⅟₂₅ scale model kit, 1970, MIB,
$75.00.

Toys

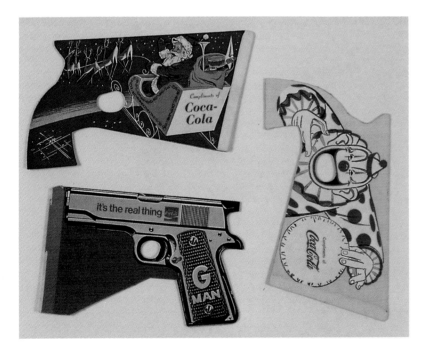

Clockwise, from top: Bang gun with Santa in sleigh, 1950s, M,
$25.00; Bang gun with clown, yellow, red, and white, 1950s,
$25.00; Bang gun, "It's the real thing," M, $20.00. Mitchell Collection

American Flyer kite, bottle at tail end of kite, 1930s,
  EX $400.00

American Flyer train car, "Pure As Sunlight," a complete train set with track and original box would push
  this price to around $4,000.00, 1930s, red and green,
  EX $1,200.00

Bank, dispenser shaped, plastic, if
this is in original box double the
price, 1960s, VG, $70.00. Mitchell Collection

Bank, bottle cap with slot in top, plastic, 1950s, M, $30.00. Mitchell Collection

Bank, dispenser shaped with glasses, add $200.00 if in original box, metal, 1950s, VG, $350.00. Mitchell Collection

Bank, plastic cooler shaped, there is a reproduction of this that has two sets of five horizontal lines on the face, plus bottles on both sides of the bottom slot, 1950s, EX, $90.00. Mitchell Collection

Bank, plastic vending machine shaped, if found in original box value will climb to $130.00, 1950s, EX, $85.00. Mitchell Collection

Bank, metal vending shaped with coin slot on top, 1940s, 2¼"x3", EX, $135.00. Mitchell Collection

Bean bag, "Enjoy Coca-Cola," with dynamic wave, 1970s, red, VG $20.00

Bicycle, EX $300.00

Boomerang, 1950s, EX $25.00

Buddy L can car, 1970s, EX $60.00

Dispenser with original glasses, "Drink Coca-Cola," 1950s, EX, $100.00. Mitchell Collection

Buddy Lee doll in homemade uniform with original patches worn by "Aunt" Earlene Mitchell's father when he worked for Coca-Cola in Paducah, Ky, 1950s, EX, $500.00. Mitchell Collection

Bus, cardboard double decker with dynamic contour logo, Sweetcentre, 1980s, red, M................... $35.00

Caboose with wave logo, 1970s, 6½" long, EX...... $45.00

Car kit, Bill Elliott's thunderboat with logo, plastic, 1:24 scale...................................... $10.00

Buddy Lee doll with plastic head, VG, $650.00. Gary Metz

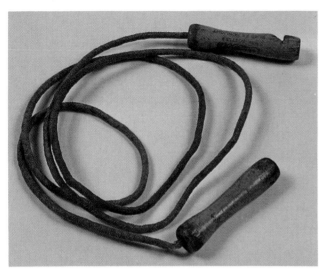

Jump rope with whistle in one handle, "Pure as Sunlight" on other handle, 1920s, G, $350.00.

Mitchell Collection

Friction car by Taiyo, 1960s, red and white, $250.00.
Gary Metz

Lionel train complete with original box and transformer, 1970s, EX, $400.00. Mitchell Collection

Car, tin Taiyo Ford taxi, friction power, "Refresh With Zest," 1960s, 9", white and red, NM. $225.00

Corvette, die cast, convention banquet gift, 1993, MRFB $20.00

Dart board with "Drink Coca-Cola" in center, 1950s, EX. $75.00

Dispenser, "Drink" on panel sides, image of two glasses over the spigot, 1960s, red and white, EX $40.00

Dispenser, plastic "Drink Coca-Cola" with dynamic wave logo on tank, 1970s, red and white, EX $35.00

"Express Cafe Snackbar," plastic and tin, "Drink Coca-Cola" button on front and advertisement on back, 1950–60s, NM. $150.00

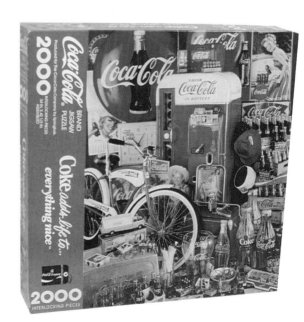

Puzzle with 2,000 pieces featuring a potpourri of Coke-Cola items, $55.00. Gary Metz

Fanny pac, Jeff Gordon shaped like pace car, logo, M . $15.00

Roller skates, embossed "Drink Coca-Cola in Bottles" on the face with "Pat. Aug 16, 1914" under first line, probably from the St. Louis Bottling Company, 1914, VG, $900.00. Gary Metz

Marbles in bag that were given away with every carton, 1950, EX $50.00

Model airplane with Coca-Cola circle for wings, 1960s, red and white, EX $40.00

Pedal car, metal and rubber, 1940–50s, 19"x36", M . $1,350.00

Pedal car, white lettering, 1940–1950, 19"x36", red, EX. $1,300.00

Picnic cooler, plastic, 6", EX $95.00

Play town hamburger stand made of wood, metal, and plaster in original box, very desirable piece, 1950s, EX $325.00

Puzzle, jigsaw in original can, 1960, EX $65.00

Puzzle, wire, with "Drink Coca-Cola in Bottles" on flat portion of puzzle, 1960s, EX $30.00

Stove, "Drink Coca-Cola with Your Meals," 1930s, green, EX $2,000.00

Tic-Tac-Toe with bottle pawns, 1950s, EX $125.00

Top, plastic, "Coke Adds Life To...Fun Times," 1970s, VG $5.00

Shopping basket, child's size with grocery graphics printed on both sides of basket liner, complete with contents, 1950s, EX, $400.00. Mitchell Collection

Yo-yo, wooden, $100.00. Mitchell Collection

Whistle, plastic, "Merry Christmas Coca-Cola Bottling, Memphis Tenn, 1950, EX $10.00

Whistle, thimble shaped, 1940s, EX $60.00

Whistle, tin, "Drink Coca-Cola," 1930, red and yellow, VG $125.00

Whistle, wood, "Drink Coca-Cola," 1940s, EX $30.00

Yo-yo, Russell Championship, "Drink Coca-Cola" on side, 1960, EX $20.00

Train tank car HO gauge, "Enjoy Coca-Cola," 1980s, EX, $35.00.

Mitchell Collection

Games

Checkers, modern, 1970s, EX, $50.00.

Mitchell Collection

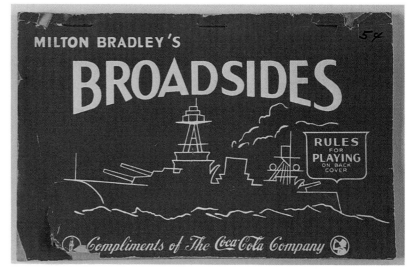

Broadsides, Milton Bradley, 1940–50s, G, $100.00. Mitchell Collection

Ball and cap game, wooden, 1960s, EX, $30.00.

Mitchell Collection

Baseball bat, 1950s, EX $175.00

Baseball bat, wooden, featuring Coca-Cola at end, 1968, EX $50.00

Baseball glove, left handed, MacGregor, 1970, EX, $175.00. Mitchell Collection

Checkers, wooden, Coca-Cola name in script on top, 1940–50s, EX, $45.00. Mitchell Collection

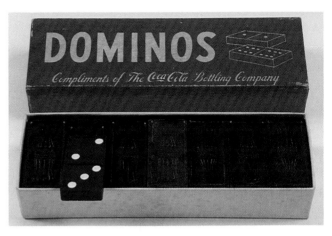

Dominos, wooden in original box, 1940–50s, EX, $55.00. Mitchell Collection

Flip game, early, showing boy drinking from a bottle with a straw, 1910–20s, VG, $850.00. Mitchell Collection

Frisbee, plastic with dynamic wave logo on top, "Coke adds life to having fun," 1960s, $10.00. Mitchell Collection

Baseball glove, left handed, 1920s, EX $350.00

Bingo card, "Drink Coca-Cola" in center spot, 1950s, EX. $10.00

Bingo card with slide covers, "Play Refreshed Drink Coca-Cola From Sterilized Bottles," 1930s, EX $45.00

Canned Wizzer Coke game, EX. $5.00

Checkers, dominos, cribbage board, two decks of cards, and a bridge score pad in a carrying box, 1940s, VG $150.00

Chinese Checkers board with Silhouette Girl logo, 1930–40s, EX. $75.00

Cribbage board, 1940s, EX. $30.00

Football, miniature, 1960s, black and white $10.00

Playing cards, top row: Spotter lady, 1943, M, $100.00; Blue wheat, 1938, M, $135.00; Great Bend, Kansas, EX, $175.00; Military nurse in uniform, 1943, EX, $135.00. Bottom: 1943, M, $100.00; "Drink Coca-Cola in Bottles," 1938, red wheat, M, $135.00; "Drink Coca-Cola in Bottles," 1938, green wheat, $150.00; Woman in uniform with wings below photo, 1943, EX, $125.00. Mitchell Collection

Playing cards, top row: Lady at party with a bottle, 1951, M, $80.00; Girl at beach, 1956, M, $75.00; Girl putting on ice skates, 1956, M, $75.00; "Refresh," 1958, M, $75.00. Bottom: Cowgirl in hat with a bottle, 1951, M, $80.00; "Drink Coca-Cola In Bottles," 1938, M, $135.00; 1943, EX, $165.00; Lady with dog and bottle, 1943, EX, $175.00. Mitchell Collection

Horse Race, in original box, EX $300.00

Magic kit, 1965, EX $175.00

Playing cards, Arkansas Chapter "Holiday Happening" in plastic, 1995, EX $30.00

Playing cards, Atlanta Christmas, 1992, EX $45.00

Playing cards, Atlanta Christmas, 1993, EX $40.00

Playing cards, Atlanta, Ga. convention cards, 1990s, NRFB $12.00

Playing cards, top row: Coca-Cola and Don Nelson of the Milwaukee Bucks, 1970s, M, $55.00; Mexico, 1971, M, $65.00; "Coca-Cola adds life to everything nice," 1976, M, $40.00; Betty, 1977, M, $30.00. Bottom: Gold box, 1974, M, $15.00; Dynamic wave trademark, 1985, M, $20.00; Girl sitting in field, 1974, M, $25.00; Bottle and food, 1974, M, $25.00. Mitchell Collection

Playing cards, top row: Santa Claus, 1979, M, $25.00; Sprite Boy and bottle, 1979, M, $35.00; "Coke Is It," 1985, M, $25.00; Red and white, 1986, M, $25.00. Bottom: Hamilton King Coca-Cola girl on the cover, 1977, M, $25.00; "Have a Coke and a Smile," double check, 1979, $35.00; Kansas City Spring Fling '82, M, $55.00.

Mitchell Collection

Playing cards, "Coca-Cola adds music to my life," 1988, EX...$25.00

Playing cards, Dearborn Convention, 1993, EX..... $25.00

Playing cards featuring a Coca-Cola bottle, 1963, white and red, EX $35.00

Playing cards featuring the bobbed hair girl, "Refresh Yourself," in original box, 1928, EX $450.00

Playing cards, top row: woman with tray of bottles, 1963, M, $55.00; Bottle on ice man, 1958, M, $75.00; Girl in pool, "Sign of Good Taste," 1959, $75.00; Couple sitting and resting under tree in planter, 1963, M, $55.00. Bottom: "Coke Refreshes You Best," 1961, M, $65.00; "Coke Refreshes You Best," girl with bowling ball, 1961, M, $65.00; Couple at beach with surf board, 1963, M, $95.00; "Refreshing New Feeling," featuring couple in front of fireplace, 1963, M, $65.00. Mitchell Collection

Playing cards, top row: model that was used on 1923 calendar, 1977, M, $45.00; "Drink Coca-Cola," party scene, 1960, M, $70.00; Beach scene, 1960, M, $85.00; Snowman in a bottle cap hat, 1959, M, $65.00. Bottom: Couple playing tennis, 1979, M, $35.00; Friends and family, 1980, M, $55.00; Couple playing tennis, 1979, M, $35.00. Mitchell Collection

Playing cards from the California Chapter of the Cola Clan, 1986, EX $100.00

Playing cards, girl in circle surrounded by leaves, in original box, 1943, EX $105.00

Playing cards, Kansas City Convention, 1995, NRFB. $10.00

Playing cards, Kansas City Spring Fling, 1993, EX . . $60.00

Playing cards, double deck in container similar to six pack holder, 1970s, EX, $50.00.
Mitchell Collection

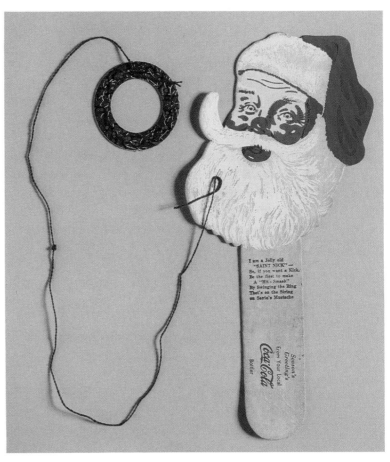

Ring toss game with Santa Claus at top of handle, VG, $15.00. Creatures of Habit

Playing cards from Campbellsville, Ky, Bottling Co, M, $65.00. Mitchell Collection

Playing cards, Elaine, 1915, EX, $1,000.00. Mitchell Collection

Playing cards, Louisville Ky. convention, 1980s,
   NRFB $12.00

Playing cards, Smokeyfest Chapter, 1994, EX $25.00

Playing cards, Smokeyfest Chapter, 1995, EX $20.00

Pool cue, dynamic wave logo, EX $55.00

Pool cue with dynamic contour logo, EX $35.00

Puzzle, bottles in tub, 1950s, 12"x18" $85.00

Puzzle, jigsaw, "An Old Fashioned Girl," in original box,
   1970–80s, NM. $15.00

Sprite Boy Double Six Domino set in original vinyl case, 1970s, EX, $25.00. Mitchell Collection

Sprite Boy ball game with glass cover and metal back, VG, $100.00. Mitchell Collection

Puzzle, jigsaw, Coca-Cola Pop Art, in sealed can, 1960, NM $12.00

Puzzle, jigsaw, Hawaiian beach, rare, in original box, NM $165.00

Puzzle, jigsaw, in original box, "Crossing The Equator," NM. $135.00

Puzzle, jigsaw, Teen Age Party, NM $75.00

Puzzle, miniature, in box, 1983, NM $12.00

Puzzle, wooden blocks that spell "Ice Cold Coca-Cola," 15", NM. $275.00

Record chart, baseball shaped, National League Hall of Fame, 1960, EX. $55.00

Shanghai, MIR $15.00

Steps to Health with original playing pieces and envelope, 1938, 11"x26", NM $130.00

Tower of Hanoi, EX $225.00

Score keeper, cardboard, keeps score of runs, hits, and errors by both teams, by score wheels, 1900s, $100.00. Mitchell Collection

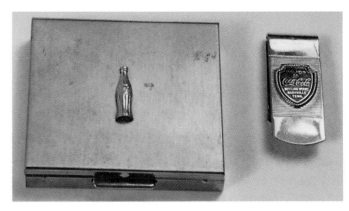

Left: Case, snap lid with raised bottle in center, all metal, EX, $75.00. Right: Money clip, compliments Coca-Cola Bottling Works, Nashville, Tenn, EX, $45.00. Mitchell Collection

Broach, "Drink Coca-Cola," EX, $35.00; Necklace with bottle, EX, $75.00. Mitchell Collection

Cuff links, gold finish, "Enjoy Coca-Cola," glass shaped, 1970s, EX, $30.00. Mitchell Collection

Charm bracelet with bottle and glass charms, EX, $125.00. Mitchell Collection

Charm bracelet, NFL with charms, 1960s, EX, $110.00. Mitchell Collection

Belt and buckle, "All Star Dealer Campaign Award," 1950–60s, M $25.00

Button, pin lock, bottle is hand club pen, VG $12.00

Coca-Cola Bottlers convention pin, shield shaped, 1912, EX. $500.00

Coca-Cola Bottling Company annual convention pin, 1915, red, white, blue, EX $600.00

Coca-Cola Bottling company annual convention pin, 1916, EX $600.00

Compact with 50th Anniversary spot on front center, 1950s, red, M $35.00

Hat pin from driver's uniform, "Drink Coca-Cola," 1930, EX. $175.00

Key chain, compliments of Coca-Cola Bottling Works, Nashville, Tenn, in original box with Merry Christmas card inside, VG, $70.00. Mitchell Collection

Key chain, 1900s, EX, $125.00. Mitchell Collection

Match safes, top: for wood matches, "Drink Coca-Cola in Bottles" on side in cameo, EX, $350.00. Bottom: "Drink Coca-Cola," F, $175.00. Mitchell Collection

Money clips, top row: gold plate with "Drink Coca-Cola" button in center, F, $35.00; "Coca-Cola" in white lettering on gold plate, EX, $30.00. Bottom: Silver plate, "Enjoy Coca-Cola," dynamic wave with knife, $30.00; "Enjoy Coca-Cola" with dynamic wave on silver plate, VG, $30.00. Mitchell Collection

Money clips, top row: bottle in horseshoe, EX, $30.00; 50th year, from the Coca-Cola Bottling Co, Piqua, OH, EX, $45.00. Key chain, bottom: 50th Anniversary, G, $20.00. Mitchell Collection

Money clip, "All Star Dealer Campaign Award," 1950–60s, NM. $20.00

Pledge pin, bottle shaped, EX $25.00

Service pin, 5 year, EX $70.00

Service pin, 10 year, EX $75.00

Service pin, 15 year, EX $75.00

Service pin, 20 year, EX $75.00

Necklace, medallion, with Hilda Clark likeness in center, 1970s, VG, $25.00. Mitchell Collection

Tie clasp, "Drink Coca-Cola," 1960s, VG, $12.00. Mitchell Collection

Watch fobs, from left: "Coca-Cola 5¢," applied paper label bottle, $50.00; 50th Anniversary, EX, $75.00; Hilda Clark in center, EX, $125.00. Mitchell Collection

Tie clasp with bottle on chain, 1940s, $30.00. Mitchell Collection

Service pin, 30 year, EX $125.00

Service pin, 50 year, as you might expect this pin is hard to find and is extremely rare, EX $375.00

Watch fob, bulldog, 1920s, EX $110.00

Watch fob, "Drink Delicious Coca-Cola in Bottles," brass with black enamel, EX $175.00

Watch fob, Duster Girl, 1911, EX $700.00

Watch fob, horseshoe shaped with paper label bottle in center, 1905, EX $950.00

Watch fob, oval, girl drinking from a bottle with a straw, 1910, 1¼"x1¾", EX $800.00

Watch fob, round celluloid girl in bonnet with red ribbon, 1912, EX $1,800.00

Wrist watch, in original metal tin, NM $35.00

Watch fob, brass, "Drink Delicious Coca-Cola in Bottles," girl drinking from bottle with straw, 1912, EX, $175.00. Mitchell Collection

Watch fob, 1915, $150.00.
Mitchell Collection

Watch fob, brass with gold wash, "Relieves Fatigue" on front, "Drink Coca-Cola Sold Everywhere 5¢" on back, 1907, EX, $150.00. Mitchell Collection

Watch fobs, from left: Brass with red enamel lettering, "Drink Coca-Cola," 1920s, EX, $150.00; Brass swastika (this was a good luck symbol until the 1930s when the Nazi connection made it an ugly form), 1920s, EX, $150.00; Brass with red enamel lettering, 1900s, EX, $135.00. Mitchell Collection

Clothing

Apron, cloth, "Be Really Refreshed" with button on chest portion, 1950s, white, VG, $30.00. Mitchell Collection

Apron with red change pockets, "Drink Coca-Cola," 1950–60s, VG, $25.00. Mitchell Collection

Apron, "Enjoy Ice Cold Coke" on bib, 1941, EX. $55.00

Apron, salesman's sample, "Drink...In Bottles," EX . $50.00

Bandanna, Kit Carson, 1950s, 20"x22", red, EX, $65.00. Mitchell Collection

Bandanna, Kit Carson, new, white, EX, $15.00. Mitchell Collection

Belt, vinyl, with "Drink Coca-Cola" blocks, 1960, white, $15.00. Mitchell Collection

Bowler's shirt, "Things go better with Coke," 1960s, EX, $20.00. Mitchell Collection

Cap, felt beanie, 1930 – 40s, 8" dia, VG, $45.00.
Mitchell Collection

Bow tie, white "Coca-Cola" on red, NM $35.00

Cowboy hat, convention, 1937, EX. $200.00

Driver's cap with hard bill, red, white, and yellow, 1930s, EX, $75.00. Mitchell Collection

Driver's shirt, short sleeve, white with green stripes and large back patch with white background, VG, $35.00. Mitchell Collection

Driver's shirt, short sleeve, 1960s, VG, $50.00. Mitchell Collection

Hat, soda person, note the term Soda Jerk wasn't coined until the 1940s, EX, $20.00. Mitchell Collection

Driver's folding cap, 1950s, $65.00. Mitchell Collection

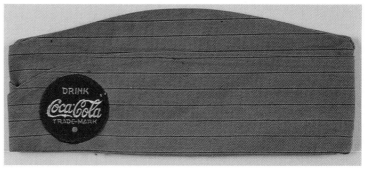

Hat, soda person, cloth, 1940, EX, $25.00. Mitchell Collection

Hat, soda person paper fold up, featuring Sprite Boy, 1950s, VG, $25.00. Mitchell Collection

Patch, small shirt, "Drink Coca-Cola," with red and black lettering, 1960s, EX, $5.00. Mitchell Collection

Kerchief, "The Cola Clan," with Silhouette Girl from Coca-Cola Collectors' banquet, 1970s, white and red, $12.00. Mitchell Collection

Patch, "Coca-Cola," red outline and lettering on white background, VG, $8.00. Mitchell Collection

Painter's hat, 1950s, F, $10.00. Mitchell Collection

Patch, "Drink Coca-Cola in Bottles" with yellow and white lettering, 1960s, red, EX, $8.00. Mitchell Collection

Patch, large, back, "Enjoy Coca-Cola," with yellow and white lettering, 1950–60s, Red, EX, $15.00. Mitchell Collection

Wallets

Left: Coin purse with snap closures, leather, arrow, "Whenever you see an arrow think of Coca-Cola," 1909, VG, $175.00. Right: Coin purse with snap closure top, leather, compliments of Coca-Cola Bottling Co, Memphis, TN, 1910 – 1920s, VG, $185.00. Mitchell Collection

Coin purse, leather with gold embossed lettering, "Drink Coca-Cola in Bottles Delicious Refreshing" with rounded metal snap top that is gold colored, 1910, black, EX . $150.00

Coin purse, leather with silver colored rounded metal snap top and silver embossed lettering, 1920s, black, EX $150.00

Embossed bottle on front, 1920s, black, EX $35.00

Leather with gold embossed lettering, 1907, black, EX. $90.00

Tri-fold with calendar and photo sleeves, leather, gold embossed lettering, 1920s, black, EX $75.00

Coin purse with gold lettering engraved in leather "When thirsty try a bottle," "Coca-Cola Bottling Company" with a paper label bottle to the left of lettering, 1907, maroon, EX, $100.00. Mitchell Collection

Trifold with calendar, leather with gold embossed lettering, 1918, black, EX. $85.00

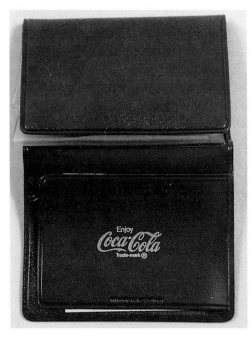

Left: Leather, black, 1920s, EX, $80.00.
Right: Leather, "Drink Coca-Cola, Delicious,
Refreshing," 1920s, EX, $30.00. Mitchell Collection

Plastic, "Enjoy Coca-Cola," 1960s,
black, EX, $8.00. Mitchell Collection

Santas

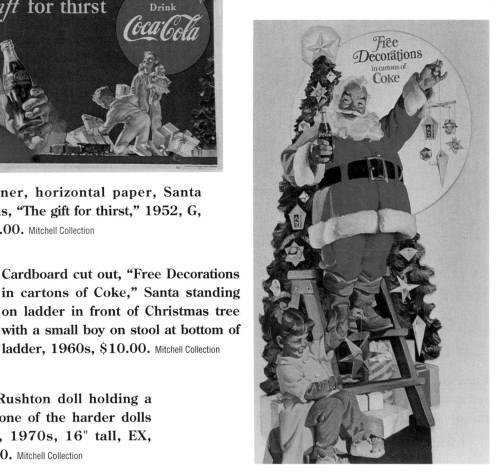

Banner, horizontal paper, Santa
Claus, "The gift for thirst," 1952, G,
$40.00. Mitchell Collection

Cardboard cut out, "Free Decorations
in cartons of Coke," Santa standing
on ladder in front of Christmas tree
with a small boy on stool at bottom of
ladder, 1960s, $10.00. Mitchell Collection

Black Rushton doll holding a
bottle, one of the harder dolls
to find, 1970s, 16" tall, EX,
$225.00. Mitchell Collection

Cardboard cut out, "Things go better with Coke," scenes of people over Santa's head, 1960s, 36", EX, $20.00.
Mitchell Collection

Cardboard cut-out showing small boy peering around a door facing at Santa who's opening a bottle, easelback, 3-dimensional, 1950s, VG, $175.00. Mitchell Collection

Cardboard stand up Santa Claus holding three bottles in each hand with a button behind Santa, 1950s, $175.00. Mitchell Collection

Cardboard stand up Santa Claus resting one arm on a post while holding a bottle with the other, a holly Christmas wreath is shown in the rear, 1960s, EX, $75.00. Mitchell Collection

Cut out Santa Claus on stool holding wooden rabbit, EX, $85.00.

Mitchell Collection

Carton stuffer Santa Claus, "Good taste for all," EX, $45.00.

Mitchell Collection

Display topper, cardboard, "Stock up for the Holidays," Santa holding a bottle behind a six pack, 1950s, EX, $125.00.

Mitchell Collection

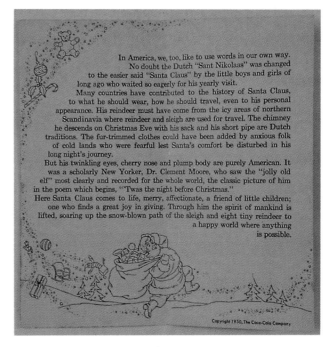

Christmas card with possible origin of Santa clothing on reverse side, $35.00. Mitchell Collection

Hanging display sign, cardboard, "Serve Coke and add Punch to your holidays," Santa at bottom of sign holding a glass, 1958, EX, $30.00. Mitchell Collection

Light hanger, 1960, EX, $12.00. Mitchell Collection

Doll, Rushton, holding a bottle, 1960s, 16" high, EX, $135.00.

Mitchell Collection

Porcelain, large animated, Santa holding a bottle and holds up a finger to quieten a small porcelain dog, New, EX, $110.00. Mitchell Collection

Porcelain, large animated, Santa holding a book that has good boys and girls list, New, EX, $110.00.

Mitchell Collection

Porcelain, large, Santa holding a bottle and a string of lights standing beside a small wooden stool with a striped package sitting on the top step, new, EX, $110.00. Mitchell Collection

Poster, cardboard, "A Merry Christmas calls for Coke," Santa seated in green easy chair while elves bring him food, 1960s, 16"x24", VG, $40.00. Mitchell Collection

Poster, cardboard, "Bring Home The Coke," Santa at his work bench, 1956, 14"x28", EX, $200.00. Mitchell Collection

Poster, cardboard, "Coke adds life to Holiday Fun," lettering on sign in front of Santa, 1960s, EX, $20.00. Mitchell Collection

Paper hanger, Seasons Greetings with Santa and helicopter, 1962, 16"x24", NM $425.00

Poster, cardboard cut out, "Free for your tree Holiday Decorations in Cartons of Coke," Santa seated at desk with a bottle, 1960s, $15.00. Mitchell Collection

Poster, cardboard, cut out, "Season's Greetings," Santa sitting in the middle of a train set with a white helicopter flying around his head, 1962, 32"x47", EX, $325.00. Mitchell Collection

Poster, cardboard, "Extra Bright Refreshment" Santa beside a Christmas tree with a six pack in front, 1955, 16"x27", VG, $50.00. Mitchell Collection

Poster, cardboard, "Get your Santa Collector's Cup," Santa holding a glass, EX, $15.00. Mitchell Collection

Poster, cardboard, "Real holidays call for the real thing," Santa holding a Christmas wreath, 1970s, 36" tall, EX, $15.00. Mitchell Collection

Poster, cardboard, vertical, "The gift for thirst, Stock up for the Holidays," children with presents and a hatless Santa with a bottle, EX, $40.00. Mitchell Collection

Poster, paper, "Coke adds life to Holiday Fun," Santa beside fireplace holding a bottle, EX, $25.00. Mitchell Collection

Poster, large, cardboard, "Holiday Refreshment Starts Here Enjoy Coca-Cola," Santa pointing to the lettering with one hand and holding a bottle with the other, EX, $25.00. Mitchell Collection

Royal Orleans porcelain figurine featuring Santa holding a bottle and looking at a globe, one part of a six series set, 1980, EX, $175.00. Mitchell Collection

Poster, paper, "The pause that refreshes," Santa in his workshop, EX, $20.00. Mitchell Collection

Royal Orleans porcelain figurine featuring Santa hushing a small dog and holding a bottle, one in a limit six part series, 1980, EX, $135.00. Mitchell Collection

Royal Orleans porcelain figurine featuring Santa seated holding a child and a bottle while a small boy kneels at a dog sitting up, one in a limited set of six, 1980s, $125.00. Mitchell Collection

Royal Orleans porcelain figurine with Santa holding a book in front of a fireplace that has a bottle on the mantel, part of a limited six part series, all 6 pieces together MIB $1,200.00, 1980s, EX, $125.00. Mitchell Collection

Royal Orleans porcelain figurine one in a limited six piece series featuring Santa sitting with a bottle while a young pajama-clad child feels his beard, 1980s, EX, $135.00. Mitchell Collection

Royal Orleans porcelain figurine featuring Santa standing beside a sack of toys and drinking from a glass, part of a six piece limited edition set, 1980, EX, $150.00. Mitchell Collection

Santa doll in black boots, original, 1950s, 16", EX, $175.00. Mitchell Collection

Sign, cardboard, double sided hanging, "Things go better with Coke," Santa and a couple kissing, 1960, 13½"x16", EX, $45.00. Mitchell Collection

Royal Orleans Santa plate, first plate, 1983, MIB $75.00

Sign, cardboard rocket, "Drink Coca-Cola Festive Holidays," die cut dimensional Santa, 1950s, 33" tall, VG, $260.00. Gary Metz

Sign, cardboard, "Santa's Helpers," Santa holding six bottles, 1950s, VG, $75.00. Mitchell Collection

Wreath, cardboard, Santa holding six bottles, 1958, EX, $20.00. Mitchell Collection

Sign, cardboard, "The More the Merrier," Santa sitting in front of Christmas tree with sacks of toys and Coca-Cola and Sprite in front of him, 1970s, EX, $30.00. Mitchell Collection

45 RPM record, Trini Lopez, with dust cover advertising Fresca, 1967, EX, $10.00. Mitchell Collection

Axe, "For Sportsmen" "Drink Coca-Cola," 1930, EX, $800.00. Mitchell Collection

Astro-Float mounts on top of bottle, designed to put ice cream in for a Coke float or ice to help cool down your drink, 1960s, VG, $15.00.

Mitchell Collection

Bookmark, paper, "Drink Coca-Cola Delicious and Refreshing" featuring Lillian Nordica at stand table with a glass, 1900s, 2¼"x5¼", NM, $1,500.00. Gary Metz

Bank, cooler style, "Have a Coke" embossed in top, 1940s, 5"x5"x3½", EX, $1,000.00. Gary Metz

Badge holder, Bottler's Conference, metal and celluloid, 1943, EX $45.00

Bell, stamped metal, "Refresh Yourself Drink Coca-Cola In Bottles" on both sides, 1930s, 3¼" tall, NM $500.00

Bolo tie, Kit Carson, neckerchief in original mailer envelope, 1950s, EX $75.00

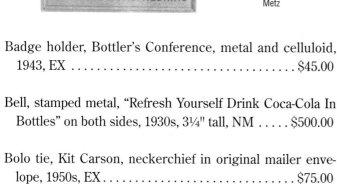

Bookmark, celluloid, "Refreshing Drink Coca-Cola Delicious 5¢," 1900s, 2"x2¼", F, $500.00. Mitchell Collection

Bookmark, celluloid, "Drink Coca-Cola at Soda Fountains 5¢," 1898, F, $550.00. Mitchell Collection

Bookmark, celluloid oval, "What Shall We Drink? Drink Coca-Cola 5¢," 1906, 2"x2¼", EX, $700.00. Mitchell Collection

Bookmark, Lillian Nordica, 1904, 2"x6", EX, $230.00.

Mitchell Collection

Bookmark with white cat, Tell City Coca-Cola Bottling Co, Inc, EX, $45.00. Antiques, Cards, Collectibles

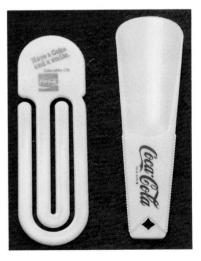

Left: Bookmark, plastic with wave logo, 1970, white and red, EX, $5.00. Right: Shoe spoon with wave logo, plastic, 1970s, white and red, EX, $8.00. Mitchell Collection

Bowl, green, scalloped edge Vernonware, "Drink Coca-Cola Ice Cold," 1930s, green, EX, $450.00. Gary Metz

Card table with bottle in each corner, advertisement sheet under side of table boasts of the fact it's so strong it can hold a grownup standing on it, 1930, VG, $225.00. Mitchell Collection

Chewing gum display box, held twenty 5¢ packages cardboard, rare, 1920s, VG, $1,500.00.

Cigarette box, 50th Anniversary frosted glass, 1936, EX, $700.00. Mitchell Collection

Comb, plastic, 1970s, red, EX, $2.00.

Chewing gum jar with thumb nail type lid, 1930s, M. $500.00   Cigar band, 1930, EX. $150.00

Counter dispenser, bolt on, 1940–50s, VG, $750.00. Gary Metz

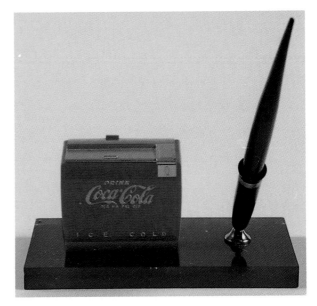

Desk pen holder with music box attached, 1950s, EX, $250.00. Mitchell Collection

Door lock, metal, "Drink Coca-Cola in Bottles, Delicious and Refreshing," 1930s, EX, $40.00. Mitchell Collection

Fact wheel, United States at a glance, EX, $75.00. Mitchell Collection

Cup, paper, red lettering "Things Go Better With Coke" on white square, 1960s, NM. $3.00

Display bottle, hard rubber, 1948, 4' tall, EX $975.00

Display bottle, plastic, with embossed logos, 1953, 20" tall, VG $210.00

Dialing finger, "It's the real thing," 1970s, EX, $15.00. Mitchell Collection

Door bar, porcelain, "Iced Coca-Cola here," yellow and white on red, Canadian, 1950s, 30", NM $200.00

Dust cover, Lone Ranger, 1971, EX $35.00

Dust cover, Superman, 1971, EX $35.00

Educational poster, chart four in the electricity series, distributed to schools for teaching aids, great graphics, but low in demand, 1940s, $15.00. Creatures of Habit

Globe, leaded glass, round, "Coca-Cola," rare, 1920s, EX, $10,000.00.

Our American Steel, poster number three in a series of four posters, great graphics but demand for educational material has remained low, 1946, EX, $8.00.
Mitchell Collection

Fly swatters, left: "Drink Coca-Cola In Bottles," EX, $90.00. Right: "Drink Coca-Cola" with net end, EX, $10.00.
Mitchell Collection

Frame for 36"x20" posters, 1940, 36"x20" , EX, $225.00. Gary Metz

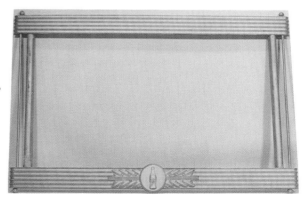

Fence post topper made from heavy cast iron, used to decorate fence pillars outside bottling plants, has a threaded base, 20" tall, EX. $500.00

Globe, milk glass, from ceiling fixture, "Drink Coca-Cola," 1930–40s, EX, $450.00. Mitchell Collection

Globe, milk glass, "Drink Coca-Cola" with trademark incorporated in tail of "C," if with original hardware add $200.00, 1930, EX, $650.00. Gary Metz

Lamp, milk glass, painted, "Coca-Cola" bottle, 1920s, 20" tall, EX, $5,500.00.

Golf divot remover, metal, EX, $25.00.

Key tag, Coca-Cola Bottling Co, Indianapolis, showing 2 cents postage guaranteed, VG, $35.00. Mitchell Collection

Flashlight in original box, 1980, EX. $20.00

Glass negative for the 1940s poster featuring the tennis girl, very unusual and rare, 20"x24", G $100.00

Ice bucket, "Drink Coca-Cola In Bottles," 1960s, EX . $15.00

Ice tong with metal handle, 1940s, EX $250.00

Ice tong with wood handle, "Drink Coca-Cola, Greencastle, Ind," 1920s, EX. $300.00

Ice tongs from Coca-Cola Bottling Co, Green Castle, Ind, has a 3-digit phone number, 1920s, EX $500.00

"Jim Dandy" combination tool that has a screwdriver, button hook, cigar cutter, and bottle opener, rare, 1920, EX $300.00

Jug with paper label in original box, 1960s, one gallon, EX. $20.00

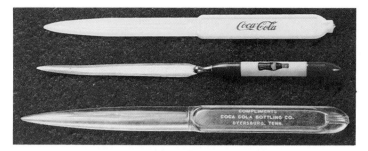

Letter openers from top: plastic, white and red, EX, $5.00; metal and plastic with bottle on handle, 1950, red and white, EX, $30.00; plastic from Coca-Cola Bottling Co. Dyersburg, Tenn, clear, EX, $15.00. Mitchell Collection

Light fixture, rectangular colored leaded glass, with bottom beaded fringe, "Coca-Cola 5¢," "Pittsburgh Mosaic Glass Co, Inc, Pittsburgh, Pa," 1910, 11"wx22"x7½"h, EX, $12,000.00.

Light shade for ceiling fixture, milk glass, "Drink Coca-Cola" with red lettering, 1930s, 14" dia, EX, $600.00.

Light, hanging adjustable, with popcorn insert on one of four sides, with red and white Coca-Cola advertising on the other panels, 1960s, 18"x18", M $525.00

Light, octagonal hanging art deco motif, believed to have been made for the San Francisco World's Fair Exhibition in 1939, 1930s, 20"w x 24"t, EX $1,800.00

Magic lantern slide, hand colored glass, "A Home Run" from Advertising Slide Co. St. Louis, 1970s, EX. . $125.00

Magic lantern slide, hand colored glass, "Good Company!" features a couple toasting with Coke bottles, 1920s, EX. $135.00

Magic lantern slide, hand colored glass, "People say they like it because...," 1920s, EX $100.00

Money bag, vinyl zippered, "Enjoy Coca-Cola," 1960s, VG, $8.00. Mitchell Collection

Magic lantern slide, hand colored glass "Stop at the Red Sign" Coca-Cola Bottling Co, Festus, MO, 1920s, EX $130.00

Magic lantern slide, hand colored slide, "Daddy-here it is," 1920s, EX. $150.00

Magic lantern slide, hand colored slide, "Unanimous good taste!," Festus, Mo, 1920s, EX $135.00

Message pad shaped like a case of Coke, 1980s, EX. . $8.00

Note pad holder for candlestick phone, price includes phone which also has a courtesy coin box, 1920s, EX, $900.00. Gary Metz

Napkin holder with Sprite Boy panel on side, "Have a Coke 5¢," 1950, VG, $700.00. Gary Metz

NCAA final four commemorative 16oz can and pin set, 1994, EX, $15.00. Gary Metz

Mileage meter with home location of Crescent Beach, South Carolina, also has bottom stamp Marion Coca-Cola Bottling Company, 1950s, VG $1,000.00

Nail clippers, samples with advertising, EX $20.00

Nail file, "Coca-Cola In Bottles" embossed in early script, metal pocket knife style, EX $100.00

Olympic disk in original box, 1980, M. $10.00

Night light, "It's the real thing" with the dynamic wave logo rectangular shaped, 1970s, EX, $25.00. Mitchell Collection

Music box, cooler shaped, in working order, 1950s, EX, $130.00. Mitchell Collection

Pen and pencil set by Cross with logo on pocket clips, in original case, M $55.00

Pen and pencil set in plastic case celebrating the 50th anniversary of Coca-Cola Bottling in Frankfort, IN, 1965, EX. $35.00

Paperweight, clear glass bottle cap shaped with "Enjoy Coca-Cola" etched in glass, M, $55.00. Mitchell Collection

Paperweight, "Coke is Coca-Cola," red and yellow, 1950s, EX, $135.00. Mitchell Collection

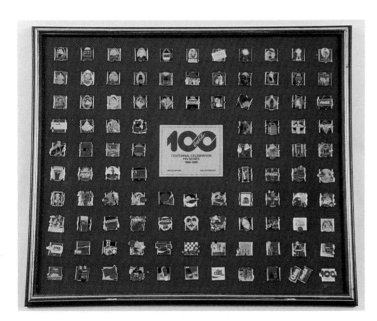

Pin set, 100th Anniversary, limited edition, framed under glass, 1986, EX, $250.00. Mitchell Collection

Pencil sharpener, cast metal in shape of bottle, 1930s, $40.00. Mitchell Collection

Pepsin gum jar with thumbnail type lid, 1910, EX, $1,600.00. Gary Metz

Pen, baseball bat shaped, 1940s, white and black, EX . $50.00

Pen, "Drink" and bottle on pocket clip, with prices for specific quantities on barrel, NM $45.00

Pen, ink, red and white, 1950s, EX $40.00

Pencil box, pencil-shaped, Sprite Boy, 1948, NM . . . $145.00

Pencil holder, celluloid, 1910, EX $135.00

Pencil holder, white with red button, 1950s, 5" tall . $300.00

Penlight, push button with wave logo, 1970s, white and red, EX, $8.00. Mitchell Collection

Pencil, mechanical, 1930s, EX $25.00

Pencil sharpener, rectangular, 1960s, EX $10.00

Pocket protector, "Coke adds life to everything nice," 1960s, white and red, $8.00. Mitchell Collection

Pocket protector, vinyl, Union City, TN, 1950s, red and black, G, $15.00. Mitchell Collection

Popcorn box, "Drink Coca-Cola," 1950s, EX, $35.00. Mitchell Collection

Polaroid camera, "Coke adds life to Happy Times," EX, $75.00. Mitchell Collection

Ruler, 12", plastic with wave logo, 1970, white and red, EX, $4.00.

Ruler, 12", wooden, "A Good Rule," very common item, 1920–1960, EX, $2.00.

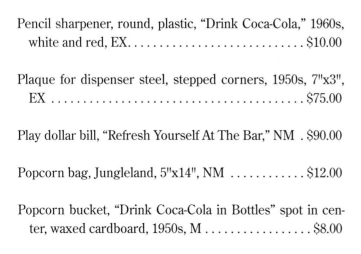

Ruler, 12", wooden, "Coca-Cola refresca en grande," 1950–60s, $5.00. Mitchell Collection

Pencil sharpener, round, plastic, "Drink Coca-Cola," 1960s, white and red, EX. $10.00

Plaque for dispenser steel, stepped corners, 1950s, 7"x3", EX $75.00

Play dollar bill, "Refresh Yourself At The Bar," NM . $90.00

Popcorn bag, Jungleland, 5"x14", NM $12.00

Popcorn bucket, "Drink Coca-Cola in Bottles" spot in center, waxed cardboard, 1950s, M $8.00

Postage stamp carrier, celluloid, 1902, EX $500.00

Pot holder, "Drink Coca-Cola every bottle sterilized," red lettering on yellow, 1910–1912, G. $275.00

Printers block with Sprite Boy, 1940s, M $25.00

Record album, "The Shadow," 1970, EX $25.00

Record carrier for 45 rpms, plastic and vinyl, 1960s, 9"x8", red and white $35.00

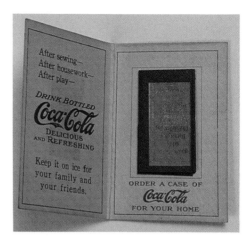

Sewing needle case with packaging featuring the same model that appeared on the 1924 calendar, 1920s, EX, $75.00. Mitchell Collection

Sewing needles in Coke packaging, featuring the girl at party with the fox fur, 1920s, EX, $75.00. Mitchell Collection

Refrigerator water bottle, green glass "Compliments Coca-Cola Bottling Co," embossed, EX, $125.00. Mitchell Collection

Shade, ceiling, milk glass with original hardware, 1930s, 10", EX, $1,500.00.

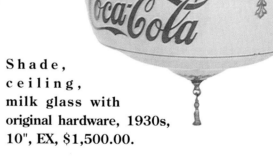

Record dust cover featuring Dick Tracy scenes and the dynamic wave, 1971, EX $30.00

Record dust cover, Sgt. Preston, 1971, EX $35.00

Record dust cover, W. C. Field, 1971, EX $25.00

Refrigerator bottle, "Compliments of Coca-Cola Bottling Company" on one side with two horses and riders on the other side, 1940–1950s, 9" tall, EX $120.00

Salt and pepper shaker, thimble shaped, 1920s, EX . $350.00

Screwdriver, pocket clip set, one straight and one Phillips blade, EX, $8.00. Mitchell Collection

Sandwich toaster, "Coke," used at soda fountains to toast sandwiches and would imprint the bread, hard to find, 1930s, EX. $700.00

School set, "Drink Coca-Cola Delicious Refreshing," complete with pencils, rulers, erasers in box, 1930s, red, EX. $75.00

Syrup dispenser, ceramic, complete, marked "The Wheeling Pottery Co," 1896, VH, $5,500.00. Gary Metz

Shade, colored leaded glass, with the chain edge that originally had a border of hanging beaded fringe, "Property of the Coca-Cola Co to be returned on demand" must be on top band, 1920s, 18" dia, EX, $4,000.00.

Statue holding bottles of Coca-Cola, "Tell me your profit story, please" on base, 1930–40s, EX, $100.00. Mitchell Collection

Tape for reel to reel for radio play, contains 16 advertising spots prepared by McCann & Erickson, Inc. New York, New York, 1970s, $25.00. Mitchell Collection

Shade, window, "Drink Coca-Cola, The Pause that Refreshes in Bottles," very rare, 4'x7', VG $3,500.00

Shotgun, model 1500XLT, Coca-Cola Centennial, embossed Coca-Cola on receiver and barrel never fired, 1986, MIB $1,100.00

String dispenser, tin, red with carton in yellow circle, 12"x16", EX $425.00

String holder, curved panels, "Take Home 25¢" six pack in spotlight, 1930s, NM $1,000.00

Syrup dispenser, reproduction, made of hard rubber, unusual piece, 1950s, EX $700.00

Street marker, brass, "Drink Coca-Cola, Safety First," fairly rare piece, 1920, VG, $175.00. Mitchell Collection

Tap knob, doubled sided, "Coke," 1960–70, NM $20.00

Tap knob, enameled double sided, "Drink Coke or Coca-Cola, Ask for it Either Way," 1940–50s, EX $70.00

Tap knob, one side, "Coca-Cola," 1970 . . . . $8.00

Tape measure, horseshoe shaped, Coke advertising on side, NM $5.00

Tokens, from left: "Free Drink, Army & Navy," new, G, $1.00; "Free Bottle, 1915 –16," new, G, $1.00; "Free bottle on demand," new, G, $1.00. Mitchell Collection

Tumbler, also used as popcorn container showing "Drink Coca-Cola," 1950–70s, EX, $8.00. Mitchell Collection

Thimbles, left: red band, 1920s, EX, $65.00. Right: blue band, 1920s, EX,, $95.00. Mitchell Collection

Wall pocket, 3-dimensional press fiber board, 9"x13", EX, $450.00. Mitchell Collection

Tokens, from left: "Free drink Atlanta, Ga," new, G, $1.00; "Free Drink 1904 Worlds Fair," new, G, $1.00; "Free Drink San Francisco Expedition," new, G, $1.00. Mitchell Collection

Water cup with handle, tin, "This cup for water but Drink Coca-Cola in Bottles, Coca-Cola Bottling Co. Greencastle, Ind" is printed in black in bottom of cup, rare piece, 1930s, EX, $125.00. Mitchell Collection

Telephone, bottle shaped, new, MIB..............$15.00

Telephone, can-shaped, new, MIB................$20.00

Telephone in the shape of a 10 oz bottle, EX $50.00

Thimble, aluminum, 1920s, EX $30.00

Thimble, "Coca-Cola," red lettering, M...........$25.00

Training kit for sales complete with record, film strips, and charts, 1940s, EX $85.00

Tumbler, tulip shaped with syrup lines, EX $25.00

Umbrella, orange, black, and white, "Drink Coca-Cola," 1930s, EX.................................$750.00

Winchester model #94, Coca-Cola Centennial, only 2,500 produced, never fired, 1986, MIB $1,200.00

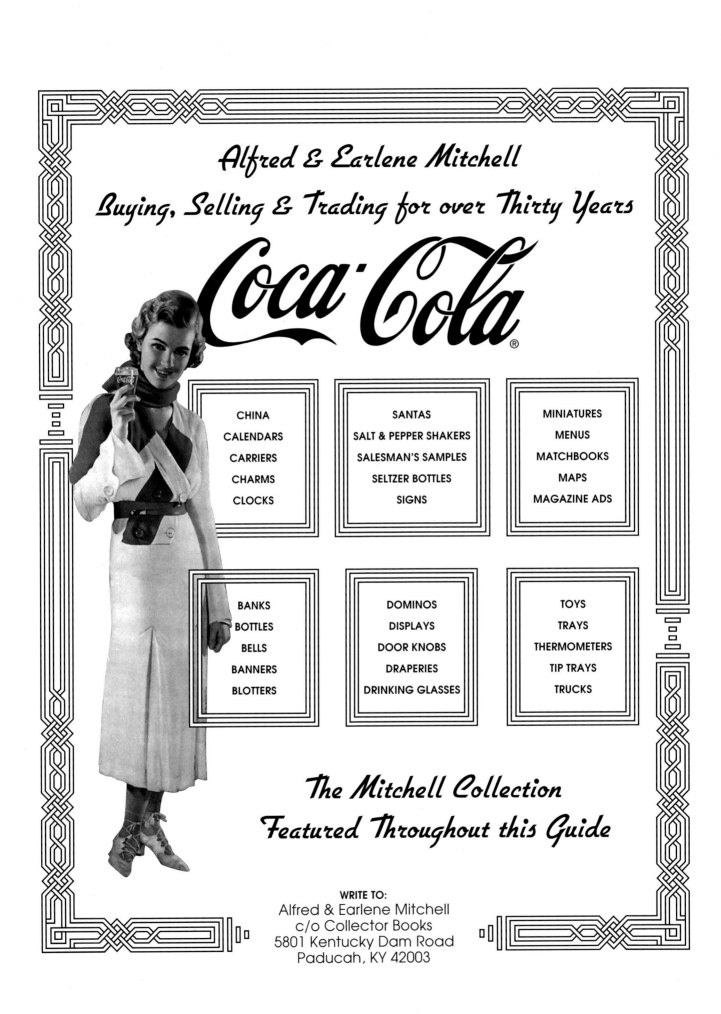